Teaching as a Profession

Sidney Dorros

Director
Publications Division
National Education
Association

Foundations of Education Series

Charles E. Merrill Publishing Company
Columbus, Ohio
A Bell & Howell Company

Acknowledgments

Much of the content of this book is drawn from a D.Ed. dissertation by the author completed at the George Washington University in 1965 under the guidance of chairman Robert E. Baker, Wesley T. Carroll, and Harry G. Detweiler.

Among many colleagues who were particularly helpful in providing information and suggestions for this book were Frank W. Hubbard, Jack H. Kleinmann, Glen Robinson, and several members of the staff of the Research Division of the National Education Association. Most contemporary writers on teaching as a profession share this author's indebtedness to the pioneer work in this field of T. M. Stinnett of the NEA, the late Albert J. Huggett of Michigan State University, Lucien B. Kinney of Stanford University, and Myron Lieberman of Rhode Island College.

Merrill's Foundations of Education Series under the editorship of Dr. Ray C. Phillips, Auburn University, and Dr. Robert J. Stalcup, The Education Commission of the States.

Library of Congress Catalog Card Number: 68-17684

PRINTED IN THE UNITED STATES OF AMERICA

Foreword

Students of the educational scene today often note the existence of strong national concern for improving the quality of education and a renewal of the historic American commitment to equalizing educational opportunities for all children and youth. Improved preparation of school personnel is a parallel, though less obvious, concern. These concerns have provided the stimulus for more rapid and more substantial improvements in education in recent years than have been achieved in any previous generation.

As might be expected, programs of preparation for professional careers in education are currently the subject of careful study, inasmuch as improving education is partially a function of improved personnel. One of the most important ways of viewing programs for preparing professional educators is two-dimensional, basic or foundational preparation and specialized preparation. The former can be conveniently defined, although perhaps the definition is an oversimplification, as being made up of content appropriate to all professional educators while the latter is that preparation which is designed to prepare a person for a particular responsibility in the profession, for example, a first-grade teacher, or a high school biology teacher, or a school superintendent. Neither dimension of preparation is adequate alone. The foundations area provides needed professional perspective, knowledge of the cultural orientation of schools, philosophical directions of education, knowledge of human growth and development, learning theory, the primary methodology of teaching, and evaluation of learning outcomes. Specialization is preparation for discharging the responsibilities inherent in the particular position one holds in the educational system.

As is true of preparation programs for other major professions, those for professional educators make use of content from several disciplines. Such content is organized according to the purposes to be served by the particular program and requires adaptations to these purposes. As implied above, preparation for careers in education relies on the disciplines of philosophy, educational psychology, sociology, anthropology, and others for its content, as well as on the discipline of education. The subject matter selected from these supporting disciplines and applied to teacher education makes up the area of professional preparation known as the Foundations of Education. Such subject matter must take form in a meaningful pattern with interrelationships of the content from the respective disciplines made clear. When this occurs, a set of useful generalizations about education, its goals, its setting, its characteristics, effective teaching and the proper evaluation of learning is possible. These generalizations are critical in the development of a professional educator and without them only educational technicians are possible.

The *Foundations of Education Series* edited by Dr. Ray C. Phillips and Dr. Robert J. Stalcup properly emphasizes this important dimension of teacher education. There is a definite and important place in professional literature for this series. It should add much to the further professionalization of preparation for careers in education.

Truman M. Pierce, Dean
School of Education
Auburn University
Auburn, Alabama

Preface

This publication, like the others in this series, is designed to give the student of professional education an overview of a specific area within the professional education field.

Keeping up with the tremendous amount of writing published each year in the field of education poses, in itself, a virtually impossible task. For this reason the authors have felt a strong need to provide students with a capsule presentation of some of the basic concepts included in the major areas of study in professional education.

The use of this series of works should serve to give the student direction in carrying on more extensive study in those areas in which he is weak. The selective bibliography included in each of these publications should provide a point of departure for any additional investigation which the student feels is necessary. In any event the authors take the position that these publications represent the minimum information which any student of education needs to have.

R. C. Phillips
R. J. Stalcup
Editors

Table of Contents

Chapter 1

Introduction

Is teaching really a profession? There are strong differences of opinion on this question.

This book is based on the assumptions that teaching *should be* a profession and that *at its best* teaching currently does meet the criteria of a profession in many respects and by many teachers. It is designed to help prospective teachers and teachers in service to develop the knowledge, understanding, attitudes, and skills necessary to achieve full professional status.

The term "teacher" in this publication refers primarily to the classroom teacher but usually includes also all instructional, supervisory, and administrative personnel in the field of education.

Criteria of a Profession

The typical dictionary definition of "profession" describes it simply as a calling or vocation, especially one that requires learning and mental, rather than manual, labor. But most writers on the subject identify several more specific characteristics of a profession. These include the following:

1

1. Concern for the welfare of society above the personal interests of members of the profession
2. Command and application of a body of specialized and systematized knowledge and skills
3. Control by practitioners of admission to the profession, standards of preparation, and performance of its members
4. A high degree of autonomy in making decisions about how to perform one's work
5. A strong professional organization which enables the group to meet the above criteria, to achieve satisfactory condi-

Figure 1

The Profession's Responsibility		The Public's Responsibility
. . . joining with the public in	establishing public policy regarding education determining purposes of education providing working conditions conducive to productivity	. . . joining with the profession in
. . . assuming autonomy for	determining and utilizing best means for achieving agreed-upon purposes ensuring competent professional personnel	. . . granting the profession the right to make and carry out decisions in
. . . joining with the public in	evaluating achievement of purposes appraising public policy regarding education	. . . joining with the profession in

Source: National Education Association, National Commission on Teacher Education and Professional Standards, *New Horizons for the Teaching Profession,* Margaret Lindsey (ed.) (Washington, D. C.: the Commission, 1961), p. 23.

tions of work, and to advance and protect the welfare of its members.

These criteria are not ends in themselves. Their major purpose is to assure that those who satisfy professional requirements are more competent to perform a particular service than anyone else. The members of any profession have the responsibility of helping to identify, develop, and maintain high standards of competence.

These criteria apply to any profession, but means of meeting them vary according to differences in the nature of the various professions. For example, many professional workers such as medical doctors or lawyers practice their professions primarily as individuals; whereas teaching is primarily a public or *institutional* enterprise. Therefore, teachers are even more dependent than doctors or lawyers upon group action to achieve and maintain professional objectives.

One of the most widely accepted definitions of the respective roles of the public and the teaching profession in making decisions about education is reproduced in Figure 1.

Professional Responsibilities

Fulfillment of the preceding roles of the teaching profession depends upon how well teachers, as individuals and as members of organized groups, perform the following ten professional responsibilities:

1. Cooperative determination of goals of education
2. Adoption, observance, and enforcement of a code of ethics
3. Research and accumulation of professional procedures
4. Education in professional procedures
5. Accreditation of professional schools
6. Recruitment, selection, and orientation of candidates for the profession
7. Certification of members of the profession
8. Maintenance of economic welfare
9. Maintenance of a desirable work climate
10. Maintenance of effective professional organizations.

These responsibilities of the teaching profession will be separately described in succeeding chapters.

Chapter 2

Goals of Education

Clearly defined and appropriate goals of education are necessary in order to plan effective instructional programs. In principle, there seems to be wide agreement with the assumption that the goals of education should be studied and defined cooperatively by the teaching profession and the public it serves. It is also widely agreed that although some fundamental values and objectives remain the same, the changing nature of society and of educational conditions make necessary continuous study and redefinition of goals. Goals of education should reflect changes in aspirations and priorities of society.

Much writing on the subject fails to distinguish clearly between determination of goals and the means of achieving such goals. This writer assumes that after the goals of education are determined in cooperation with the public, the profession itself should have autonomy in determining the best *means* of education to achieve the agreed upon goals.

History of Determination of Goals of Education

1. Religious Influences

a. Religion played a dominant role in the European education from which our American system of education evolved. Prior to the 18th century, most European education could have been described as being of, by, and for the church.

b. Colonial Massachusetts, a leader in developing the concept of public education for all, was a theocratic state in which the Puritan religion was linked closely to the government. Therefore, early education in Massachusetts had three main goals: (1) to teach all citizens enough to read the Bible, (2) to instill moral and religious precepts, and (3) to prepare a small number of learned men to perpetuate the faith as ministers or lay church and community leaders.

c. Strong religious influences prevailed in both public and private education in many states until well into the 19th century. In the early years of that century there was strife over the "common schools" in cities of mixed population, such as New York. Catholics objected to what they considered to be indoctrination in Protestant dogma in the schools. This was one of the reasons for the establishment of Catholic parochial schools.

d. The provision in the United States Constitution for separation of church and state slowly influenced states to eliminate sectarian religious instruction from the public schools in favor of nonsectarian moral and democratic principles.

2. Influence of Prominent Individuals

a. Benjamin Franklin was an exponent of emphasis in education on preparation for real life, including vocational preparation.

b. Thomas Jefferson advocated a few years of free basic education for all citizens to enable them to function as enlightened citizens and to raise the level of their economic competence, with advanced education only for the most able students to prepare them for positions of leadership.

c. Horace Mann, often referred to as "the father of American public schools," was a lawyer and member of the Massachusetts State Legislature before his famous career as the first secretary of the Massachusetts State Board of Education from 1837 to 1849. He popularized and applied concepts of secular schools and the perfectability of man through education.

d. John Dewey, famous worldwide for his advocacy of pragmatism in education, was an academic philosopher before he made his mark in shaping the goals of education.

e. University presidents, through writing and speaking, have had great influence in shaping the goals of American education. The most prominent in recent years has been James B. Conant, former president of Harvard. In his book *Shaping Educational Policy*, published in 1964, Conant declared that there was need for *nationwide* educational policy even though he was opposed to centralized *national* control of education.

3. Governmental Influences

a. Following the American Revolution, authority over education was vested in most states by provisions of state constitutions. Much of this authority was delegated to county, city, and district school boards; but basic goals of education were often written into state law or determined by state school boards.

b. The federal government, even before the substantial federal aid to education legislation of the mid-sixties, had more significant influence on the goals of education than is generally recognized. For example:

(1) In 1787, the Continental Congress, in setting aside lands in the Northwest Territories for the support of education, declared that "religion, morality, and knowledge being necessary to good government and the happiness of mankind, schools and means of education shall forever be encouraged."

(2) The objective of education for vocational competence has long been fostered by federal legislation such as the Morrill Act of 1862, supporting agricultural and technical education in "land-grant colleges;" and the Smith-Hughes Act of 1917, initiating federal support of vocational education.

(3) The National Defense Education Act of 1958 clearly supported the goal of advancing and protecting the national interest through education.

(4) The Elementary and Secondary Education Act of 1965

had as its major goal the elimination of poverty through education.

4. The Influence of the Teaching Profession

a. Practicing educators had little influence in formulating goals of education until their professional organizations had become recognized and respected by the public.

b. The reports of several study committees of the NEA beginning in the 1890's influenced the goals of education at all levels.

c. The most influential statement of educators on the goals of education was expounded by the NEA Commission on the Reorganization of Secondary Education. Its policy statement, *Cardinal Principles of Secondary Education,* was published in 1918. It defined seven major goals of education: health, command of fundamental processes, worthy home membership, vocational ability, civic competence, worthy use of leisure, and ethical character. This statement was a major influence leading to the development of the comprehensive high school. The same goals have been applied also to elementary and junior high schools and, to a more limited extent, to college curriculums.

d. In 1935, the NEA and its Department of Superintendence (now the American Association of School Administrators) formed the Educational Policies Commission (EPC) to prepare, publish, and disseminate statements of proposed policy regarding the conduct of education in the United States. Members of the twenty-member Commission have been distinguished educators chosen by the sponsoring associations but entirely free to make their own recommendations based upon extensive study and consideration. The policies advocated by the Commission do not automatically become policy of the NEA or AASA but have received serious consideration by many educational bodies and generally found great acceptance. The scope of problems studied and reported on may be seen in the following sampling of reports of the Commission:

The Purposes of Education in American Democracy (1938)
Education for All American Youth (1944)
Moral and Spiritual Values in the Public Schools (1951)
Higher Education in a Decade of Decision (1957)

Contemporary Issues in Elementary Education (1960)
The Central Purpose of American Education (1961)
Universal Opportunity for Education Beyond the High School (1964)
American Education and the Search for Equal Opportunity (1965)

e. Numerous other organizations of educators have influenced the goals of education. These include the predecessor to the EPC, the NEA-sponsored National Council on Education; the Progressive Education Association; the National Society for the Study of Education; the NEA Association for Supervision and Curriculum Development, and many other specialized professional organizations. The American Council on Education has been particularly influential in the field of higher education.

Present Means of Determining Goals of Education

Current means of determining goals of education are extremely complex, involving almost all Americans in some way. Most state constitutions vest responsibility for education in the state government; but, traditionally, the legislatures have delegated major direct control of goals of education to state and local boards of education. However, the formal, observable means of determining goals may not always be the most significant. Many social and educational powers operate indirectly, behind the scenes, or through interaction.

1. State and Local School Boards

a. State school boards and departments of education vary greatly in the degree of leadership they provide in shaping the goals of education, but most state boards do outline major goals within which local boards must operate.

b. Most citizens seem to consider their local school board to be the basic agency for official determination of goals of education. Since the members of school boards are elected, or appointed by elected officials, their decisions ultimately reflect the weight of public opinion in each school district. School boards are also strongly influenced by the recommendations of the school staff, particularly the superintendent of schools. Ideally, the school board serves as a catalyst for combining the thinking of laymen and educators in framing educational goals. Some state and local boards establish, or cooperate with, citizens' advisory committees or joint committees of laymen and educators who study and make recommendations regarding school policy.

c. The influence of teachers on local school board policies is achieved indirectly by the influence of individual teachers and their organizations on public thinking. And, to a great extent, teachers teach according to their own values and goals.

2. The Federal Government

a. Legally the federal government has no direct control over goals of education. But, as indicated earlier, from the beginning of our nation the federal government has sought to influence educational goals as they relate to the national welfare. Currently there are three major means by which the federal government influences educational policies in the state and local school systems:

(1) Categorical federal financial aid to education, designed to support only specific kinds of educational programs, clearly support goals such as providing equal educational opportunities for all Americans or strengthening the quality and numbers of scientists, engineers, and technicians for national defense.

(2) Various government agencies, especially the U. S. Office of Education, influence goals of education by dissemination of information or exhortation.

(3) The federal government influences school policies indirectly through national legislation and judicial decisions on social problems such as civil rights and child labor.

3. Professional Organizations

In addition to the means of influencing goals outlined in the history section of this chapter, professional organizations of educators currently have significant influence on educational goals in the following ways:

a. Policy platforms and resolutions of general and specialized education associations—local, state, and national—are usually revised annually. This process provides a focus for consideration of educational goals and, after adoption, sometimes has considerable influence on the thinking of the teaching profession and, to a more limited extent, upon the public. The most comprehensive and influential national policy statement of this kind is the Platform and Resolutions of the National Education Association. Long-term goals, revised only occasionally, are contained in the Platform. Resolutions dealing with more specific current issues are discussed, modified, and adopted by the NEA Representative Assembly each summer at the annual convention of the NEA. The Platform and Resolutions of the NEA are to be found in the *NEA Handbook* published each fall.

   b. Lobbying activities of education associations often influence goals of education, especially at the state level.

   c. Professional literature provides a forum for discussion and dissemination of information and ideas related to the goals of education.

4. Mass Media

   Professional communications about education are often over-shadowed by national and local newspapers, magazines, radio, television, and popular books. These media are giving increasing attention to education and are influencing the thinking of educators as well as the general public.

5. Higher Education

   Colleges and universities influence goals of education in at least four ways:

   a. The basic values instilled in all college students affect the goals of education that they will seek or support as voting citizens.

   b. Teacher preparation programs at colleges and universities shape the goals of educators.

   c. Some individual professors exert considerable influence on the public, the profession, school boards, and legislatures through consultation, speeches, and publications.

   d. The most important influence of colleges and universities on goals of education is achieved indirectly by the standards of admission to college and the nature of higher education curriculums.

Since increasing proportions of the nation's youth seek higher education each year, there is tremendous pressure upon secondary, and even elementary schools, to pursue as educational goals whatever learnings will help gain admission to higher education. Thus the goals of all levels of education are closely related.

6. Philanthropic Foundations

Money "talks" in influencing educational policies by large educational foundation grants for studies and projects. For example, the work of James Conant in influencing educational goals was financed by the Carnegie Corporation and dissemination of the recommendations of the NEA Project on Instruction was supported in part by the Ford Foundation (Fund for the Advancement of Education). The two aforementioned foundations are currently the most influential in the field of education.

Problems and Issues in Determining Goals of Education

1. Effects of a Pluralistic Society

The great variety of races, religions, national and cultural backgrounds, occupations, geographical and economic conditions in the United States helps to create many diverse concepts of the goals of education.

2. Is Local Control of Education Mythical or Meaningful?

Some analysts of educational policymaking conclude that the influence of local school boards is relatively small in comparison with the influence of other groups referred to earlier in this chapter. The contention is that although school boards may go through the motions of defining goals of education, they usually adopt policies in conformance with state and national influences. Factors that foster state, regional, and national influence on educational goals are listed below.

a. The communities of our nation are becoming increasingly interdependent.

b. Our population is extremely mobile.

c. The dominant means of communication which help shape

public thinking are national in scope, such as radio and television networks, mass-circulation magazines, and mass-marketed books. Even local newspapers use national wire services and nationally distributed features.

d. Local school districts often lack the financial resources to implement desirable goals.

e. Politically, it is usually easier for special interest groups to "capture" control of local policy-making bodies than of state or national governmental or professional leaders.

3. Should the Schools Build a New Society?

Contending educational philosophies argue in favor of three different approaches to the determination of school goals: (1) perpetuating the heritage of the past, (2) meeting the needs of the present, and (3) laying the foundation for a better society in the future. Although the greatest publicity is usually given to the avid advocates of exclusive attention to any one of these approaches, in actual practice our educational goals currently tend to be influenced by all three criteria.

4. Difficulties in Assessing Achievement of Educational Goals

If they are to be meaningful, we need to know whether and how educational goals are achieved. This is difficult to accomplish because:

a. Most goals are stated in terms of "behavioral objectives," whereas most assessment instruments such as standardized tests are based primarily on knowledge. In the 1950's and 1960's, significant progress was made in developing more effective means of evaluating achievement of educational goals. The continuing work of Benjamin Bloom, David Krathwol, and others toward developing a "Taxonomy of Educational Objectives" seeks to classify educational goals in precise terms which can be used in devising means of evaluation as well as in planning curriculums to achieve desired outcomes.

b. Since education affects the entire lifetime of individuals, the achievement of some objectives may not be observed until many years after the educational program which was intended to induce the desired behavior. More long-range evaluation of the effects of education is needed to determine how well educational goals are achieved.

Outlook for Determination of Goals

1. Local, State, and National Cooperation

It appears likely that organizations and government at all three levels will be partners in determining educational goals. Federal financial aid, while increasing national influence on goals, is also providing the economic means to strengthen state departments of education and to free states and local school systems from the educational straight-jackets formerly imposed on them by lack of adequate funds to pursue desired goals.

2. Continuous Study and Adjustment

Rapidly increasing technological, economic, political, and social changes will require continuous and extensive adjustment of educational goals and priorities among them.

3. Increasing Participation of Teachers in Determining Goals

It appears likely that classroom teachers and other educators will find greater involvement in policy-making in the future for the following reasons:

a. The increasing complexity of conditions influencing education will require greater expertise than most laymen have.

b. Higher standards of preparation for teachers will increase their ability and desire to share in policy-making.

c. General trends toward democratization of the means of making decisions in many aspects of life will apply to educational policy-making as well.

d. Increasing recognition of teaching as a profession and more flexible instructional materials will give individual teachers, teams of teachers, and entire school faculties greater opportunity to shape goals for their own teaching.

e. The increasing strength and activity of teachers' organizations will enable them to exert greater influence on issues upon which there is general agreement among members of the profession.

What Teachers Can and Should Do About Goals of Education

1. Direct Roles

a. All teachers should help influence the climate of public opinion by dissemination of information and opinion on educational matters through individual discussions with parents and through civic and social contacts.

b. Every teacher should be able to participate rationally in the formulation of goals for his own classroom, school, or school system.

2. Indirect Participation

a. Indirect participation in the formulation of goals can be achieved by supporting and helping to shape objectives of local, state, and national professional organizations.

b. Active exercise of citizenship rights to participate in politics will be increasingly important as education has been, and will increasingly be, subject to political control in the broadest sense.

3. Background for Making Decisions

To make wise decisions about educational goals teachers need to acquire, in addition to professional knowledge and skills, broad knowledge and understanding of:

a. Our total culture through a "liberal education."

b. The relationship of general social problems to education.

Chapter 3

Code of Ethics

Every profession, including education, needs a code of ethics to guide its members to high standards of practice and to protect the profession and the public from detrimental behavior.

History of Codes of Ethics for Teachers

1. State Codes

The first code of ethics applicable to a large group of educators is reputed to have been adopted by the Georgia State Teachers Association in 1896. Several other state associations adopted codes around the turn of the century.

2. National Code

The first national code of ethics of the teaching profession was adopted by the National Education Association in 1929. Minor revisions were made in 1939 and 1941, and a major revision was adopted in 1952.

3. Lack of a Common Code

By 1960, thirty of the sixty-four state associations affiliated with the NEA and a number of local associations had adopted the NEA Code of Ethics. But thirty-four state associations and many local associations had formulated their own codes. Many teachers who moved from the state in which they had prepared to teach found a different code of ethics in effect in their new state.

4. Adoption of "Code of Ethics of the Education Profession"

Major efforts to develop a universally accepted, enforceable code were begun by the NEA Committee on Professional Ethics in 1961. Following widespread consideration and discussion throughout the nation, representatives of most state education associations affiliated with the NEA; many departments and a number of other professional organizations met in a national conference to discuss and modify the Committee proposals. The resulting "Code of Ethics for the Education Profession" was approved by the NEA Representative Assembly in 1963. This Code applies to all educators, regardless of position, and is organized under the following four principles:

Principle I: Commitment to the Student

Principle II: Commitment to the Community

Principle III: Commitment to the Profession

Principle IV: Commitment to Professional Employment Practices

The complete text of the Code of Ethics of the Education Profession is available from the NEA.

Present Status of Professional Ethics

1. Acceptance

By 1966, all state associations and twelve national departments of the NEA had adopted the Code of Ethics of the Education Profession. These organizations represent about ninety percent of all American public elementary and secondary school teachers and an undetermined smaller proportion of private school and college teachers.

2. Implementation

Most activities to implement the Code of Ethics are positive in nature. Local, state, and national association ethics committees, or committees dealing with professional rights and responsibilities, seek to disseminate information about the Code, interpret its provisions, and stimulate observance of ethical standards. Adherence to the Code of Ethics is a condition of membership in the NEA and many of its affiliated associations.

a. The local association, because of the individual relationships involved in observing the Code of Ethics, has the most direct role in implementation of the Code. An active local ethics committee, or other committee serving this function, provides information and interpretation informally as well as in formal written and oral presentations. Most alleged violations or questions about interpretation of the Code are resolved amicably and privately by the local committees.

b. The state association provides leadership training programs for ethics committees and supplements interpretation of the Code through publication of articles in the state journal and through individual counsel where necessary. It also serves to investigate alleged major violations of the Code which the local association is unable to handle.

c. The national ethics committee of the NEA provides leadership in revising the Code and interpreting the application of various parts of the Code to specific types of professional problems. These are published as they develop in the *NEA Journal* and other professional journals and in periodic additions to a cumulative record of such interpretations in the NEA booklet, *Opinions of the Committee on Professional Ethics.* The 1966 edition of this publication contained fifty opinions on ethical aspects of specific activities such as selling encyclopedias, participating politically in school board elections, and reporting teacher grievances in the press.

3. Enforcement

Only as a last resort is punitive action taken to enforce professional ethics. Means of enforcement by professional associations of ethical behavior include private or public censure and suspension of or expulsion from association membership.

Current Issues

1. Legal Status

In most states the Code of Ethics has no legal status. The Ethics Committee of the NEA has advocated "legal recognition that adherence to the Code as it is interpreted by the profession is a recognized condition for maintaining a certificate and continuing contract."

2. Application to Nonmembers

The Code of Ethics was drawn to apply to all educators; but there is dispute as to how it can, or whether it should, apply to teachers who are not members of the NEA or its affiliates that have adopted codes of ethics. At the time of writing of this book about seven percent of all public school teachers were members of the American Federation of Teachers which had not developed or adopted any code of ethics; and a relatively small number of teachers did not belong to any teacher organization.

3. Additional Codes for Special Groups Within the Profession

The Code of Ethics of the Education Profession was intended to apply to all members of the profession, in all levels and in all types of schools; but a number of groups, such as school superintendents, have felt a need to formulate their own codes, in addition, to relate specifically to their specialized responsibilities. Also, many teachers in higher education do not look upon the Code as relating to them.

Outlook for Ethics

1. Enforcement Machinery

It seems likely that the National Education Association and its state and local affiliates will develop more effective formal machinery whereby flagrant violations of professional ethics will result in disciplinary action. Such enforcement will include legal channels as well as association channels.

2. Teacher Rights

Increased emphasis will be given to rights of teachers as well as to ethical responsibilities.

3. Review of the Code

There will be continuing study, reconsideration, and possible modification of the Code of Ethics. When the Representative Assembly of the NEA adopted the "Code of Ethics of the Education Profession" it provided for review of the Code every five years "for the purpose of keeping it up to date to meet the needs of a dynamic profession."

What Teachers Can and Should Do About Ethics

Every teacher should be prepared to take the following responsibilities:

a. To be thoroughly familiar with and observant of the Code

b. To help frame association machinery for implementation of the Code and for handling infractions

c. To help build a climate for adherence to the Code and to recognize and cope with violations of the Code

d. To participate in periodic evaluation of the Code.

Chapter 4

Research

One of the major reasons for lack of full recognition of teaching as a profession has been the scarcity of valid research relevant to professional procedures. Organized research in professional procedures in education is relatively new and underdeveloped.

In the past, educational research has been minute compared to research in the natural sciences, industrial development, or some other professions such as medicine. While many industries were spending between five and ten percent of the total operating budget during the early sixties for research, less than one-half percent of all public funds spent for education were devoted to research. But in recent years massive support of educational research by the federal government promises to provide much more definitive knowledge about the learning process. Thus, participation in and knowledge of educational research is becoming increasingly important to all teachers and students preparing to teach.

History

1. Recent Development of Educational Research

Until the beginning of this century, teaching procedures were based mainly upon tradition, accumulated observations and experiences, and intuitive judgments. There was little organized research until the turn of the century, with no substantial development until the second decade of the century. Most research was confined to studies of very limited scope by individuals or small groups at universities. Some studies were carried out by small research units in the larger city school systems.

2. The American Educational Research Association

By 1915, there were enough city directors of research to form the National Association of Directors of Educational Research. In 1930, it became the American Educational Research Association. The Association itself did not conduct research, but stimulated and improved research through exchange of information among research practitioners and through dissemination of research findings to all interested practitioners through publications such as the periodical *Review of Educational Research* and the *Encyclopedia of Educational Research.*

3. The NEA Research Division

In 1922, the NEA initiated a Research Division which has grown to be the largest nongovernmental research organization in the field of education. Most of the studies conducted by the Research Division have been survey-type studies. They have described actual conditions in education, including patterns of school organization, finance, facilities, curriculums offered, and teaching conditions. This information, in addition to its direct use, has helped supply basic data for studies by other researchers. Shortly after its founding the Division began to issue the *Research Bulletin* on a regular basis.

4. What Research Says to the Teacher

In 1939, the publication by the NEA Department of Classroom Teachers (DCT) of *Implications of Research for the Classroom*

Teacher foreshadowed an era of increased dissemination and application by classroom teachers of research findings. In 1953, the DCT and the American Educational Research Association initiated a continuing series of brief pamphlets to interpret the findings of research for application in the classroom. This "What Research Says to the Teacher" series has been credited with major influence in moving research from theory to practice. The series paralleled increased dissemination and application of research findings by other specialized professional organizations such as the Association for Supervision and Curriculum Development (ASCD).

5. Action Research

Beginning in the 1940's, the ASCD gave leadership to a movement called "action research", in which large numbers of teachers are directly involved in identifying problems, forming hypotheses, experimenting with new approaches, and applying research findings. Such activity proved to be more valuable as a means of inservice education than as a means of research.

6. The USOE Cooperative Research Program

The Cooperative Research Program, launched by the U.S. Office of Education in 1954 (but not funded until 1956) provided the most important source of stimulation and assistance to educational research in recent years. This program provides grants for educational research on a great variety of problems. For the fiscal year of 1967 alone Congress appropriated $70 million for Cooperative Research. Considerable additional funds for educational research were made available through other federal programs and agencies.

Present Status of Research

1. Role of Universities

Most of the research grants under the Cooperative Research Program have gone to university-based researchers, many of whom are psychologists and members of professions other than teaching.

2. State and Local Research

Larger numbers of school systems and state departments of education than ever before are involved in trying out or demonstrating new ideas in teaching. Much of the support for such activity comes from programs initiated or expanded in 1965 by the federal Elementary and Secondary Education Act and the Higher Education Act.

3. Roles of Professional Organizations

The primary roles of professional organizations of teachers are:
a. To seek adequate support for research
b. To disseminate information about research findings
c. To serve as "watchdogs" to see that various kinds of research programs are soundly conceived and carried out
d. To participate directly in conducting research.

Current Issues and Problems

1. Shortage of Trained Educational Researchers

The tremendous increase in research funds in recent years has not been matched by similar increases in the numbers of qualified personnel to spend the funds most effectively.

2. Gap Between Theory and Practice

Lack of effective communication between theorists and practitioners often prevents most effective application of research findings. This is due in part to these factors:
a. The shortage of educational researchers has brought many people into educational research from fields other than education. Some educators believe that researchers with no training or experience in teaching do not understand the problems and needs of education.
b. Many educational researchers do not consider it to be their task to interpret or apply research findings to existing conditions in the schools.
c. Many educators do not understand the esoteric language of some researchers.

3. Confusion Between Research and Demonstration

Some of the projects labelled as "research" are really demonstrations of ideas based upon hunch or inadequately tested hypotheses. If it is really to "prove" anything, research must provide for adequate controls, take into account all significant variables, draw appropriate samples, and be evaluated objectively.

4. Effects of Research Upon Participants

Research in many other fields deals with expendable materials. Researchers in the natural sciences and technology are accustomed to many more failures than successes in testing hypotheses; however, students and teachers are not expendable. Teachers and administrators must be on their guard to see that proposed research projects are well planned, do not make unreasonable demands upon students and teachers, and have expected outcomes of sufficient value to justify the effort. To make such a judgment the teacher needs to be familiar with at least the fundamental principles of good research, and to carry out an adequate program of research in education many more highly competent researchers than are now available are needed.

Appropriate involvement of large numbers of students and teachers in research projects is essential to the advancement of the quality of education and to meet changing conditions in technology, social organization and other aspects of life.

Outlook for Research

1. Increasing Application of Research to Education

There is no doubt that teachers in the future will be involved more than ever in the conduct and application of research.

2. Expanded State and Local Research

Some provisions of federal legislation are specifically designed to encourage state and local research activity. Additional funds will probably be appropriated by state and local agencies.

3. Faster Dissemination of Information About Research

Microfilm, microfiche, computerized informational storage and retrieval, and other technological devices will supplement and partially replace printed and person-to-person communication.

4. Continuous In-Service Education of Teachers

Rapid accumulation of knowledge about the learning process and the content of education will make lifelong study of professional procedures and content essential for all teachers. It seems likely that local school systems, state departments of education, the U.S. Office of Education, and professional organizations will play increasing roles in in-service education, often in partnership or mutually supportive programs.

What Teachers Can and Should Do About Research

All teachers should:

a. Learn enough about research methods to be able to interpret implications of research for teaching, to identify problems that need study, and to participate upon occasion in group or individual research activities

b. Maintain an attitude conducive to lifelong learning of new developments in research

c. Support and encourage the conduct of research by most agencies related to education.

Chapter 5

Teacher Education

Every profession requires education in specialized professional procedures in addition to broad general education and education in the content of the professional field. In the majority of professions, practitioners exercise control of or share in determining the nature of professional preparation. This is a major means of maintaining high standards for the profession. In the field of education such a role is relatively new.

History of Teacher Education

Prior to the 1830's, there was practically no special preparation for teachers, most of whom were temporary or part-time instructors. Special preparation for teaching was first stimulated by the rapid expansion of public education and by the influence of European efforts to develop principles of pedagogy and to train teachers for their work. Progress in teacher education has been slow; and, since its inception, there has been great difference of opinion and practice in regard to the objectives and methods of preparing teachers. Generally, the education of teachers has tended to reflect prevailing goals of the schools and concepts of the learning process.

1. Normal Schools

Special training for elementary school teaching preceded such preparation for teaching at the secondary level.

a. The first attempt to provide a special program for the preparation of elementary school teachers is believed to have been made about 1785 by Samuel McCorkle at the Zion Parnassus Academy, a private school in North Carolina.

b. The first academy in the north especially devoted to teacher preparation was founded by Samuel Hall in Concord, Vermont, in 1823. The principles and techniques of teaching espoused by Hall were published in 1829 in his *Lectures on Schoolkeeping.*

c. The first public institution for teacher education was established in 1839 in Lexington, Massachusetts. Horace Mann and James Carter were especially influential in getting the Massachusetts legislature to authorize and support this pioneer venture. It and similar schools following it came to be known as "normal schools" after the French *école normale,* since they were modeled to a great extent on teacher preparation schools in France and Prussia. The principles of learning and teaching espoused by the Europeans Herbart and Pestalozzi were especially stressed in the early normal schools.

At first, the normal schools were primarily post-elementary schools with no fixed standards for admission. They slowly evolved higher standards until, when they became the dominant type of institution for preparation of elementary school teachers early in this century, they offered the equivalent of two years of college education.

2. Chairs of Pedagogy

The establishment of professorial chairs of pedagogy at some universities was a major step in achieving professional preparation of teachers. The University of Iowa is reputed to have established the first permanent chair of pedagogy in 1873. Within the next two decades such chairs were established at the public Universities of

Michigan, North Carolina, and Indiana, and at the private universities, Johns Hopkins, Cornell, and New York University.

3. Teachers Colleges

a. Separate college-level institutions especially for the preparation of elementary and secondary teachers began to develop in the latter part of the nineteenth century.

b. Two of the first colleges established primarily to prepare teachers were the George Peabody College for Teachers (1875) in Nashville, Tennessee, and Teachers College (1889), Columbia University, in New York City. These two colleges helped create greater "academic respectability" for professional preparation of teachers and were widely imitated by other colleges and universities.

c. Teachers colleges increased slowly in numbers during the first part of the twentieth century until, by the 1930's, they were the major type of teacher preparation institution. Many two-year normal schools evolved into four-year colleges. During the same period many universities added schools or departments of education.

d. Teachers colleges were instrumental in reducing some of the great differences previously prevalent in the preparation of elementary and secondary school teachers. The normal schools that had prepared elementary school teachers emphasized methods of teaching and a review of elementary school subjects, while the colleges and universities preparing high school teachers placed almost exclusive emphasis on subject matter. The comprehensive teachers college added teaching methodology to the preparation program for secondary school teachers and more advanced study of academic disciplines to the preparation of elementary school teachers.

e. The most rapid growth of teachers colleges came after World War I. A major stimulating factor was the rapid increase in high school enrollment during the twenties and thirties, creating a severe shortage of teachers by the forties. Simultaneously, there was a spurt of research and reporting of research findings in fields related to education, particularly in educational psychology and tests and measurements. The activity of educational philosophers such as John Dewey also helped provide content for formal, college-level education in professional procedures.

4. Comprehensive Colleges and Universities

a. By the 1960's, almost all teachers colleges had converted to general colleges or universities that offered a wide variety of programs.

b. The main factors accounting for the conversion of teachers colleges to all-purpose institutions include:

(1) A demand for more college facilities to take care of increasing numbers of college students in all fields

(2) Increasing "academic respectability" for teacher preparation

(3) The advantages to students of the greater depth and breadth of general and specialized education available in a comprehensive institution.

Current Status of Teacher Education

1. Numbers and Types of Preparatory Institutions

a. Approximately 1,200 colleges and universities are engaged in teacher education. These comprise slightly more than half of all higher education institutions in the United States. More college students prepare for teaching in elementary and secondary schools than for any other single field of work.

b. Teacher preparation institutions vary widely in their nature and in the types of programs they offer. In 1964, according to Armstrong and Stinnett's *Manual on Certification Requirements,* the numbers of institutions in various categories were as follows: [1]

General or liberal arts colleges	777
(197 public and 580 private)	
Universities	261
(116 public and 145 private)	
Junior colleges	50

[1] W. Earl Armstrong and T. M. Stinnett, *A Manual on Certification Requirements for School Personnel in the United States,* 1964 ed. (Washington, D.C.: National Commission on Teacher Education and Professional Standards, National Education Association, 1964), p. 22.

Teachers colleges	47
(35 public and 12 private)	
Technical schools	29
Unclassified schools	9

c. Although the private institutions outnumber the public institutions, the larger size of the public colleges and universities accounts for their production of about two-thirds of the graduates prepared to teach in elementary and secondary schools.

d. The nature of the educational programs offered in the different types of teacher preparation institutions depends to a great extent upon their origins and history of development, and upon the prevailing standards for teacher certification and institutional accreditation.

2. Nature of a Good Teacher Preparation Program

Basically, there are three components of the theoretical aspect of teacher preparation: general education, specialization, and professional education. In addition to the theoretical studies, preparation programs include student teaching and other direct experiences, usually in the senior year of college. The New Horizons Project described professional education as including:

a. Knowledge of human behavior; of work in areas of mental, emotional, social, and physical development of children and youth; of the psychology of learning; and of adjustment and personality development

b. Knowledge of how to work with others in effecting curricular changes and of how the part of the curriculum with which the educator is concerned relates to the total educational program

c. Knowledge of teaching methodology and selection and use of instructional materials to make the educator most effective in his chosen area

d. Ability to act as an intelligent consumer of educational research and to engage in practical experimentation

e. Responsibility as a member of a vital profession

f. Continuous preparation for intelligent participation in community life as a spokesman for education and as a private citizen

g. Consideration of social forces that bear on education and development of the ability to make wise decisions and to carry out constructive leadership.

In-Service Education of Teachers

1. Need for In-Service Education

Since the inception of professional training for teachers, in-service development after teachers begin teaching has received great attention. The conditions that have required in-service education include the following:

a. Employment of persons who have inadequate preparation for teaching

b. Rising standards of teaching and preparation during the career lives of teachers

c. Varying conditions, philosophies, and procedures in different school systems

d. Rapid growth of knowledge in almost all fields in which schools offer instruction

e. New knowledge of the learning process

f. New instructional materials and devices

g. Changing economic, technological, political, and social conditions.

2. Major Means of In-Service Education

Major means and sources of in-service education are:

a. Courses at colleges and universities

b. Institutes and workshops

c. Professional association conferences and conventions

d. Professional literature

e. School faculty meetings

f. Internships

g. Informal help from other teachers, principals, and supervisors

h. Educational travel

i. Teacher participation in framing of goals, curriculum, research, and the solution of school instructional and organizational problems.

Major Current Issues in Teacher Education

1. How Important Is Study of Professional Procedures in Preservice Preparation of Teachers?

a. Some public figures and academic scholars have criticized the amount of time devoted to professional education, particularly so-called "methods courses." They have urged greater emphasis on liberal education and upon the content of the subject or subjects to be taught. Some have maintained that most teaching procedures can be best learned from experienced teachers in supervised practice teaching and teaching internships. This viewpoint is usually based on the assumption that there is little valid theoretical foundation upon which to base programs of instruction.

b. Proponents of substantial preservice professional education maintain that there is a valuable body of knowledge pertinent to teaching, much of it developed in relatively recent years. They point to other professions, such as medicine, in which considerable theoretical study and laboratory experiences precede actual practice in the internship.

2. How Long Should the College Program for Prospective Teachers Last?

Conant and others have expressed the opinion that four years of college are sufficient for elementary and secondary school teachers. The NEA TEPS Commission and other professional groups advocate at least five years of college for regular elementary and secondary teachers and at least six years for specialists and college teachers.

3. What Should Be the Nature of In-Service Education?

There is general agreement that continuous in-service study and growth of teachers should be accomplished in many ways; however, most state and local school system policies tend to encourage only formal course work taken for credit at a college or university. Many state regulations require elementary and secondary teachers to take some course work periodically in order to retain certification. Most state and local salary schedules offer extra pay for advanced course work or higher degrees.

Often, no evaluation is made of the appropriateness for a particular teacher of the course work selected or of the effect of such work on the teacher. It is argued that this situation encourages teachers to make expediency a major factor in selection of courses and that it encourages the proliferation of courses of mediocre value in many colleges and universities that have nearly "captive" teachers as graduate students.

4. Should Prospective College Teachers Receive Specific Preparation for Teaching?

Traditionally, college teachers have received no special preparation for teaching. Mastery of a subject field and ability to do research and writing in one's field have comprised the main requirements for positions in higher education. But there is increasing pressure to provide for the *teaching* as well as the *scholarship* functions of college teachers. This pressure is based on (a) the assumption that effective teaching at any level is governed by the same basic learning principles and (b) the observation that many college faculty members who are competent scholars and researchers are poor teachers, particularly at the undergraduate level.

Trends in Teacher Education

1. Longer Preparation

There is a clear trend toward providing five years of college preparation for elementary and secondary teaching.

2. All-Institution Concern for Teacher Education

There is a strong movement away from exclusive program planning by "education professors" alone to cooperative planning involving representatives of the faculty members of academic subject fields.

3. Specialized Preparation in One Field for Elementary School Teachers

At least two factors seem to point in this direction:

a. Changing patterns of elementary school organization and instructional procedures are creating demands for teachers with specialized training.

b. Some groups, such as the NCTEPS, have advocated intensive study of one special field as a means of developing the values of scholarship for prospective elementary as well as high school teachers.

4. Development of the Internship

Increasingly, preparatory institutions and school systems are providing internship in addition to student teaching. The internship differs from student teaching in at least three ways:

a. It generally follows the four-years preservice preparation program.

b. The intern assumes full responsibility for at least one-half to three-fourths of a teaching load.

c. The intern is paid for his work.

What Teachers Can and Should Do to Improve Teacher Education

1. Feedback

After gaining some classroom experience the individual teacher can provide valuable information to his preparatory institution by reporting his evaluations of the effectiveness of various aspects of the college program in preparing him for teaching.

2. Group Policy-Making

The most significant roles of the teacher in influencing the nature of teacher education are achieved indirectly through participation in determining and supporting policies of state and national professional associations in all of the interrelated aspects of professional standards. These include accreditation of preparation programs, and certification, recruitment, and selection of teachers.

3. In-Service Education

Teachers have considerable opportunity to influence in-service education in at least three ways:

a. Through direct participation in individual and group in-service education activities

b. Through support of professional association activities, such as conferences and publications, that provide opportunities for in-service education

c. Through seeking and accepting informal assistance from other teachers, supervisors, and administrators and offering assistance to colleagues, particularly new teachers.

Chapter 6

Accreditation

Accreditation of professional schools plays a major role in raising and maintaining professional standards in teaching. It is a process whereby a recognized agency evaluates and approves the program and facilities of preparation institutions according to specified standards.

Teacher education is accredited on three levels: state, regional, and national. Accreditation procedures, particularly at the national level, are relatively new and are evolving rapidly from the historical backgrounds outlined below.

Ideally, accreditation should assure the prospective teacher that an approved institution will provide him with a satisfactory and acceptable education. It also should protect the public from unqualified teachers and the members of the teaching profession from discredit which incompetent colleagues might bring them. Colleges and universities benefit also from sound accreditation procedures that help improve their educational programs and that build confidence in the approved institutions.

Historical Development of Accreditation

1. State Approved Programs

Beginning about the middle of the nineteenth century, state education agencies were given the authority to approve teacher preparation programs within the state. One of the first such legal provisions was an 1849 New York State Law providing that a diploma from the state's normal school constituted evidence that the holder was a qualified teacher.

2. Regional Accrediting Agencies

a. Regional accrediting of higher education has its roots in accrediting of high schools by colleges interested in assuring themselves of high caliber students. The University of Michigan began to evaluate high schools in 1871. Graduates of approved schools were admitted to the university without examination. By the end of the nineteenth century regional associations of colleges had formed throughout the country for the main purpose of setting standards for high schools.

b. The North Central Association of Colleges and Secondary Schools drew up the first regional standards for liberal arts colleges in 1909 and published its first list of accredited institutions in 1913. Other regional associations soon instituted similar practices.

3. Accreditation of Professional Schools

a. The medical profession has led the way in accreditation of professional schools. A special council of the American Medical Association began to evaluate medical schools in 1907. The work of this agency was stimulated and facilitated by publication, in 1910, of the now famous report by Abraham Flexner, *Medical Education in the United States and Canada.* Flexner revealed alarmingly low standards and inadequate programs in more than half the medical schools then in existence. Many "diploma mills" were eliminated and the quality of medical training and the status of doctors was enhanced through strict accreditation standards developed and enforced by the AMA. Several other professions established accrediting procedures for their fields before education followed suit in 1927.

b. The American Association of Teachers Colleges combined accreditation with membership requirements beginning in 1927. The membership of this organization was limited to normal schools and teachers colleges and did not include teacher preparation programs offered in universities and liberal arts colleges.

c. In 1948, the AATC merged with other associations to form a more inclusive organization, the American Association of Colleges for Teacher Education (AACTE) which continued to accredit members of the organization. Considerable progress in advancing standards was made through this self-governing type of accreditation; however, there were severe limitations upon the program. By 1954, AACTE had on its rolls only 284 of the more than 1,100 institutions which were preparing teachers at the time. More importantly, the status of the teaching profession in general and of teacher preparation programs in particular was widely criticized at the time as grossly inadequate.

d. In order to give a voice in accreditation to elementary and secondary school teachers as well as other interested groups, and to achieve a more universally acceptable accreditation procedure, the National Council for Accreditation of Teacher Education was formed in 1952. In 1954, it took over the list of institutions affiliated with AACTE and began work to re-evaluate those colleges and additional institutions upon request. The NCTEPS of the NEA played a major role in forming the new organization.

Current Status of Accreditation of Teacher Education

Although still fraught with problems, national accreditation of teacher education institutions is a widely accepted reality as evidenced by these facts:

1. By 1966, 426 teacher preparation institutions had been accredited by NCATE. These institutions prepared more than 70 percent of the new teachers entering the profession.

2. Reciprocity among the states in teacher certification has been greatly facilitated by NCATE accreditation. More than half the states grant regular certificates to teachers who have completed teacher education programs in any institution accredited by NCATE, thus making it

easier for teachers to cross state lines to accept positions.
3. Coordination with regional accreditation of colleges is achieved by the requirement that applicants for NCATE accreditation must hold regional accreditation.

Problems and Issues in Accreditation

1. Should There Be National Accreditation at All?

a. In 1963, James B. Conant stimulated vigorous national debate on this question when he recommended in his book, *The Education of American Teachers*, that national accreditation of teacher education be eliminated altogether. He proposed instead, that each institution recognized by state authorities as a "legitimate" college or university should be permitted to develop whatever program of teacher education it considered most desirable within a few broad guidelines administered by the state. He proposed to relegate only advisory roles to the accrediting bodies.

b. Conant's proposals seemed to be based upon the premise that, except for carefully supervised student teaching, little special professional preparation for teaching is necessary.

c. The major arguments against Conant's proposal, which seem to have prevailed, include the following:

(1) Adequate preparation for teaching does require considerable specialized academic study in addition to that provided by a liberal arts education program.

(2) Almost all other major professions have found it necessary and beneficial to have national accreditation programs.

(3) The mobility of our population and of teachers makes minimum national standards highly desirable.

(4) Political and economic pressures make it difficult for state agencies to enforce high standards. Proponents of this argument point to the fact that almost all institutions purporting to prepare teachers, many of which have grossly inadequate programs, have been able to get approval from the state in which they are located.

2. Who Shall Control National Accreditation?

Basically, there are three types of accrediting agencies among the thirty or so professions that accredit professional schools:

(a) associations of practitioners, (b) associations of professional schools, and (c) joint councils including representatives of practitioners, professional schools, and legal licensing agencies. NCATE falls into the joint council category, but, since its inception, there has been a struggle over the relative representation on the Council of practicing teachers and representatives of the preparatory colleges and universities.

The Outlook for Accreditation

Although controversy over details will continue into the predictable future, it seems likely that national accreditation of teacher education is here to stay. It will probably be responsible for the following developments during the careers of present and prospective teachers:

1. Virtual elimination of weak teacher preparation programs.
2. Higher standards and improved programs in remaining preparation programs.
3. Almost complete reciprocity among the states of teacher certification based on accreditation standards.

What Teachers Can and Should Do About Accreditation

1. Indirectly, all teachers can help shape and support accreditation policies through membership and participation in their professional organization represented in NCATE.
2. Teachers should help create a favorable climate for accreditation, including the expectation that new teachers be prepared at accredited institutions.
3. In advising prospective teachers regarding choice of a college, educators should point out the advantages of attending an institution that has full accreditation: state, regional, and national.
4. Teachers should select fully accredited institutions for their own advanced study.
5. A limited number of teachers will have the opportunity to participate directly on NCATE evaluation teams.

Chapter 7

Recruitment, Selection, and Orientation of Teachers

Every teacher has a personal stake in the selective recruitment and orientation of new teachers because the reputation of the entire profession is shaped by the performance of each member thereof. Furthermore, every teacher should have enough concern for the welfare of students to motivate him to relp recruit good prospective teachers, to discourage or block admission of poor prospects to teaching, and to help new teachers succeed in their work.

History

1. Teacher Participation in Selective Recruitment

The desirability of teacher participation in the selection of prospective colleagues was stated as long as 1858 by the second president of the National Education Association, Zalmon Richards; but little was done in a formal way to implement this idea until relatively recent years.

2. Future Teachers of America

The Future Teachers of America (FTA), at first including both high school and college chapters, was founded by the NEA in 1937 to help recruit teachers and orient them toward the understanding of teaching as a profession.

3. Student National Education Association

The Student National Education Association was established in 1957 for college students preparing to teach.

Status of Recruitment, Selection, and Orientation

Most formal recruitment, selection, and orientation activities are conducted by administrative, supervisory, and guidance personnel of school systems and by the faculties and placement officers of colleges and universities that prepare teachers. However, classroom teachers, as individuals and through their organizations, also play important roles in these processes.

1. Teacher Influence

Studies show that the influence of individual teachers is significant in shaping decisions of students to seek to become teachers and that new teachers rate very highly the value of help and suggestions given to them by other teachers.

2. FTA Program

In 1966, there were over 6,400 chartered FTA chapters in United States high schools, each guided by a faculty sponsor and supported by the NEA and affiliated state and local associations. The FTA program is, to a great extent, an exploratory program. It provides information and experiences to help members decide whether they have the abilities and interests needed to become successful teachers.

3. Student NEA Program

By 1966, there were approximately 1,000 Student NEA chapters, one in almost every teacher preparation institution, with a total membership of about 120,000. Student NEA activities develop understanding of the teaching profession and of the history, ethics, organizations, policies and programs of local, state, and national professional associations.

4. Subject Field Student Organizations

Other student programs designed to help recruit, select, and orient teachers in specific teaching fields such as music, business, and science, are sponsored by subject area associations of teachers.

Problems and Issues in Selective Recruitment and Orientation to the Profession

1. What Are the Characteristics of a Good Teacher?

Recruitment and selection of high quality teachers is handicapped by the fact that research has not yet identified with certainty criteria upon which to base a definition of a good teacher or personal characteristics that will make a good teacher. However, the research that has been done and the intuitive judgments of educators do provide some working guides for selecting good prospects for teaching. The NCTEPS, in its 1963 *Position Paper on Teacher Education and Professional Standards,* stated that students wishing to enter and remain in teacher education programs should meet high standards on the following counts: [1]
  a. Intelligence
  b. Academic achievement
  c. Physical stamina and health
  d. Emotional stability
  e. Moral and ethical fitness
  f. Knowledge of correct spoken and written English
  g. Ability to work with others.

2. Are Good Teachers Made or Born?

It is sometimes said that good teachers are those who have "nat-

---

[1] National Education Association, National Commission on Teacher Education and Professional Standards, *A Position Paper on Teacher Education and Professional Standards* (Washington, D.C.: the Commission, 1963), p. 7.

ural ability" for teaching. The opposite of this viewpoint seems to be held by some teacher preparation institutions which do not screen potential teachers carefully for basic traits that are important in teaching. It is no doubt true that good teachers are made *if* they bring to their teacher preparation those basic traits that make teaching an art as well as a science.

3. Need for Experience to Prove One's Ability to Teach

Demonstrated success in working with students is essential to determine whether a person will make a good teacher. Some teacher preparation programs do not provide any directed teaching experiences until the senior year of college. In such cases, many students fail to learn that they don't really have the ability or the desire to teach until their college program has been completed. To avoid such a belated rude awakening, early exploratory experience in working with students is provided in high school by FTA programs and early in college programs through the regular curriculum or through Student NEA.

4. Great Variances in Supply and Demand for Teachers

Many prospective teachers, having heard of a general shortage of teachers, incorrectly assume that shortages exist in all fields and in all school systems. This is far from true. Conditions vary greatly by school system, school level, and subject.

The Outlook for Teacher Supply and Demand

1. No Shortage in Some School Systems

Competition will be keen for teaching positions in school systems or colleges that offer high pay and desirable working conditions. It will continue to be difficult for a new teacher to get a position in such a school system or college without first proving his abilities in a less favored school or college.

2. Imbalance In Preparation for Elementary and High Schools

Nationwide, the shortage of elementary teachers is likely to continue to be much greater than the shortage of high school teachers, because a much higher proportion of college students are preparing to teach at the high school level than at the elementary level. In 1965, when elementary school teachers were needed in the ratio of 9 to every 6 secondary school teachers, the numbers of students preparing to teach were in the inverse ratio.

3. Differences by Secondary School Subject Field

Some secondary school teaching fields may actually be over-supplied. In the following fields there were more teachers prepared in 1965 than there were new public school positions available that year: agriculture, art, biology, commercial education, home economics, industrial arts, music, men's physical education, social studies, and speech. An insufficient number of graduating students were prepared in the following subjects: English, foreign languages, general science, library service, and mathematics.

However, in interpreting this information, it is important to know that in the country as a whole only about sixty-eight percent of four-year college graduates prepared to teach in secondary school actually enter teaching immediately after graduation. Also, the percentage of graduates entering different teaching fields varies greatly by subject. For example, although an adequate number of graduates are prepared to teach in home economics, the field, being exclusively supplied with women, has a high rate of attrition and turnover creating a shortage of home economics teachers in some communities.

4. Junior High School

The junior high school, which combines traditional elementary and secondary school levels, will continue to be a "no-man's land" in some communities, suffering from a greater shortage of *qualified* teachers than either elementary or senior high schools.

5. Colleges and Universities

In practically every field of higher education the demand for adequately prepared teachers in the foreseeable future will exceed the supply. This situation is likely to continue for some time because high birth rates have increased the numbers of college-age persons in the United States, and larger proportions of this age group are entering college and are continuing in higher education for longer periods of time than previously.

6. Junior Colleges

The rapid growth of two-year junior or community colleges has siphoned off many high school and college teachers and promises to require many more teachers in the future.

7. Nonteaching Personnel

At all levels of education there will be shortages of adequate personnel for administrative, supervisory, research, and other professional, nonteaching positions.

8. Impact of Federal Aid

New and expanded school programs, stimulated especially by federal aid to education, will continue to create a demand for many types of specialized teaching personnel heretofore employed on a limited scale or not at all. There will be need for many more teachers in early childhood education, teachers prepared especially to work effectively with disadvantaged students, reading specialists, remedial teachers of various kinds, guidance counsellors, and other specialists.

9. Sources of Information About Teacher Supply and Demand

To keep up with changing developments in teacher supply and demand, prospective teachers, teachers in service, and counsellors will find useful the latest editions of the NEA Research Division reports, *Teacher Supply and Demand in Public Schools* and *Teacher Supply and Demand in Universities, Colleges, and Junior Colleges.*

What Teachers Can and Should Do About Selective Recruitment and Orientation

1. Direct Influence

a. Of course, the major direct responsibilities for recruiting, selecting, and orienting teachers are delegated to the faculties of teacher preparation institutions and to administrators and supervisors of schools and colleges. Many school systems hold special orientation sessions prior to the opening of schools and some continue in-service programs for new teachers through the school year. However, all teachers have the opportunity and the responsibility as members of a profession to help recruit and orient able new colleagues.

b. Studies show that the influence of individual teachers is significant in shaping decisions of students to seek to become teachers, and that many students decide to become teachers early in their school lives. Every teacher from kindergarten through college, whether he is conscious of it or not, influences recruitment and orientation to the teaching profession by his own behavior as a teacher.

c. Large numbers of teachers have opportunities to exert direct influence on prospective and new teachers through guidance and counseling, sponsorship of FTA or Student NEA chapters, work with student teachers, or advising and assisting new teachers informally.

2. Indirect Influence

a. Every teacher has an opportunity to help indirectly to recruit and orient new teachers through supporting activities and publications of professional associations to serve these purposes. In addition to sponsorship of FTA and Student NEA, professional associations conduct orientation programs and publish information of particular interest to prospective and new teachers in newsletters, journals, handbooks, and other publications.

Chapter 8

Certification of Teachers

Certification is the process of giving legal approval to an individual to practice his profession. For teachers this is usually done by state departments of education, often with the advice or direct participation of representatives of the profession in establishing standards of certification. As is the case with other aspects of professional standards, the major purposes of certification are (a) to help enhance the quality of education by permitting to teach only those who are qualified and (b) to protect the teaching profession from unfair job competition from improperly prepared or incompetent teachers.

History of Teacher Certification

1. Local School Boards

Local certification by a lay school committee, based on an oral examination of the candidate for a specific teaching position, was the typical pattern of licensure for public school teachers until the last quarter of the nineteenth century.

2. State Departments of Education

Certification responsibility gradually moved to county and then state levels. By the 1950's, almost all teacher certification in the United States was vested in state departments of education, professionally administered, but with policy controlled by lay boards of education.

3. Low Standards

Until after World War II teachers had little voice in the establishment of standards for certification. In 1945, just before the start of the professional standards movement, teacher certification standards were extremely varied from state to state, generally lower than deemed desirable by professional leaders, and subject to modification or evasion through frequent issuance of emergency credentials.

a. There were practically no provisions for reciprocity of certification on a national basis.

b. Only eighteen states required a minimum of a bachelor's degree for certification of elementary school teachers.

c. Approximately fourteen percent of all public school teachers held emergency certificates.

4. TEPS Commission

In 1946, the NEA established the National Commission on Teacher Education and Professional Standards. One of the first actions of the Commission was to advocate the bachelor's degree as the *minimum* level of preparation for any teaching position. The work of the NCTEPS and state TEPS Commissions helped to accomplish dramatic advances in certification requirements by the 1960's.

Current Status of Teacher Certification

Certification requirements are quite complex and constantly changing. The most authoritative and comprehensive information on this subject is to be found in *A Manual on Certification Requirements for School Personnel in the United States,* published by the National Commission on Teacher Education and Professional

Standards of the NEA. It is revised every three years. The certification requirements summarized below are those in effect in 1966 as far as they could be determined from the 1964 edition of the *Manual on Certification Requirements* and later information from various other sources. For details regarding specific current requirements in any state it is advisable to write to the state department of education of that particular state.

1. Who Is Required to Hold a Certificate?

a. All states now require public elementary and secondary school teachers to have a certificate or license to teach. These are almost always issued by state departments of education except for a few large cities such as Baltimore, Buffalo, New York, and Portland that have the authority to issue their own licenses to teachers.

b. In twelve states, teachers in public junior colleges are required to hold certificates.

c. Four states require state college teachers to hold certificates. In all cases the provisions apply to teachers colleges or state colleges evolved from teachers colleges.

d. Only sixteen states require teachers in private schools to be certificated, in some cases only at certain levels. However, in slightly more than half the states, private school teachers must meet the same requirements as public school teachers if their schools are to receive accreditation by the state.

2. Types of Certificates

There are many types and titles of certificates, even within a given state. The NCTEPS *Manual on Certification Requirements* classifies them as indicated here:

a. According to term or duration of validity: (1) life, (2) permanent, (3) limited, (4) continuing, and (5) provisional or probationary.

b. According to levels of preparation: (1) regular, (2) standard, (3) professional, and (4) emergency or substandard.

c. According to teaching position or assignment: (1) blanket or general, with no area, teaching field, or subject specified on the certificate; (2) endorsed, with each authorized teaching area, field, or subject endorsed on the certificate; and (3) special-field, with either a separate certificate for each special field or one certificate on which separate special fields may be endorsed.

3. Preparation Requirements for Certification

The preparation requirements for certification fall into three major categories: (a) total amount of higher education, (b) amount and nature of professional education, and (c) amount and nature of study in the content of a teaching field. These requirements vary according to school level and teaching field. The preparation must be taken in an institution or program accredited by the state or, as is allowed in more than half the states, in a college anywhere in the country accredited by NCATE. Often the state agency will accept the recommendation of an institution that offers a state-approved teacher education program as evidence that a particular candidate has met the preparation requirements.

a. High school teachers are required to have at least a bachelor's degree in all states and elementary school teachers must meet this requirement in forty-five states and the District of Columbia. Five years of preparation are required by at least ten states for full certification of secondary school teachers and by eight states for elementary school teachers. In some of these states the fifth year may be completed within a specified period after initial certification. Administrators and supervisors are required to have at least a master's degree in most states and six years of higher education in some.

b. Professional education requirements vary widely, ranging from sixteen to thirty semester hours, with an average of twenty-three hours, for elementary school certificates and from twelve to twenty-nine, with an average of nineteen semester hours, for secondary school certificates. These figures include from two to eight credits for student- or directed-teaching experience.

c. Requirements for study in the content of a teaching field or fields vary greatly according to the state and according to different fields within a state.

(1) For elementary school teachers, except in special subjects such as art or music, there is generally no requirement for study in depth of any single subject.

(2) For certification of high school teachers, the required semester hours of study for a typical field of teaching such as English vary among states from fifteen to forty hours for a major field credential and from nine to thirty-six semester hours for a minor field credential.

4. General Requirements for Certification

In addition to varying preparation standards according to teaching fields, all states require candidates for teaching positions to meet certain general requirements regardless of teaching field. General requirements may require all prospective teachers to:

a. Meet stated standards of age, citizenship, or health

b. Formally declare loyalty to the United States and/or the state

c. Study certain prescribed courses such as the history of the state and/or the United States

d. Be recommended by the institution that prepared them

e. Pay specified fees.

5. Emergency Certificates

Although their number is decreasing, most states still issue emergency certificates to teachers who do not meet the regular certification requirements. Such certificates are variously labelled by terms such as "provisional" or "temporary." Usually an emergency certificate is issued only when a fully qualified teacher cannot be found for a particular position. Often an emergency certificate may be converted to a regular one after a teacher meets the preparation requirements through study while teaching.

6. Qualifying Examinations

Examinations are not widely used as a basis for certification; however, a few states and large cities require passage of a test in addition to preparation requirements and some use proficiency tests in place of part of the preparation requirement. Some states also issue different grades of certificates according to scores on a given examination. In such cases teachers receiving required scores are paid more than those who do not make the minimum score. The most widely used examination for these purposes is the National Teacher Examination.

7. Certification Renewal

Some states require periodic course work or other in-service study for renewal of certification.

8. Role of Professional Advisory Councils and Committees

Almost all states have advisory committees or councils made up of representatives of the teaching profession to advise the state education agencies regarding provisions for teacher education and certification.

Issues and Problems in Teacher Certification

1. Lack of Professional Control in Determining Certification Standards

Although professional educators have significant influence in determining certification standards in all but a few states, the control over such standards is legally held by laymen on the state board of education or the state legislature. Many other professions have greater direct authority to determine standards of licensure through state licensing boards composed of professional practitioners. Some educators urge that similar authority be given to the teaching profession. Some propose separation of licensure and certification so that licensure would constitute admission to the profession and be controlled by professional practitioners, and certification by a state or local agency would be limited to serve only to regularize conditions of employment and remuneration of public school personnel.

2. Quantity vs. Quality in Certification Requirements

Most certification requirements are designated in terms of degrees, credit hours, and other quantitive standards. Standards of quality are almost entirely the responsibility of the colleges and universities. Many representatives of higher education, such as James B. Conant have held that this is as it should be. But others have observed that many teacher preparation institutions have low standards. The following two procedures have been suggested as means of helping to assure licensing only of high quality teachers:

a. More rigid accreditation standards coupled with programs to improve teacher education

b. Requirement of passage of qualifying examinations in order to receive certification. The examples of examinations for licensure of other professionals such as doctors and lawyers are often cited as support for this viewpoint. Reasons given for opposition to examinations include the contentions that it is difficult to measure teaching abilities through examinations and that examinations would tend to stultify improvement of teacher preparation by encouraging colleges to "teach for the exam."

3. Amount of Professional Course Work Required

During the 1950's and 1960's there has been considerable pressure to reduce the number of so-called "methods" or "education" courses required for teacher certification. See the section on issues in teacher education in this book for arguments pro and con.

4. Certification Differences Among the States

Remaining differences in certification requirements from state to state cause great difficulties for many teachers, some of whom teach in several states during their careers. In some cases the differences are slight but still require additional course work for new teachers in a state. Substantial differences in requirements tend to create substantial differences in the nature and quality of instruction offered in the states.

a. Arguments advanced in favor of greater similarity of standards in all the states center around:

(1) The increasing mobility of people in the United States

(2) The concern that all children should receive an adequate education no matter where they live

(3) The increasing interdependence of all areas of the United States which makes quality education valuable to the entire nation and poor education a serious detriment to the national interest.

b. Arguments in favor of diversity of certification requirements include:

(1) Traditional pride in states' rights

(2) Great social, economic, and political differences among the states

(3) The alleged flexibility and opportunities for innovation fostered by varying standards.

5. Detrimental Effects of Emergency Certificates

a. The use of emergency certificates has helped to put a "warm body" in every classroom in periods or areas of severe teacher shortages. Many people so certified have been good teachers, but many others who have not been adequately prepared have caused harm to students and to the reputation of the entire teaching profession.

b. Use of the emergency certificate has also allowed some school systems to avoid raising salaries or to improve teaching conditions enough to attract fully qualified teachers.

c. It is contended that elimination of emergency certificates entirely would force improvement of educational programs as well as enhance the status of the teaching profession.

The Outlook for Teacher Certification

It seems likely that during the next few decades certification procedures will move in the directions outlined below:

1. Widespread adoption of the requirement of five years of higher education required for certification to teach at any level

2. Greater similarity of certification requirements among the states and increased reciprocity

3. Increased use of examinations as part of the basis for certification

4. Greater depth of concentration in high school subject fields and requirements for elementary teachers to study in depth at least one subject or specialized field

5. Greater influence on and control of certification and/or li-

censure by legally recognized professional standards boards composed of representatives of various segments of the teaching profession

6. Improved procedures for rescinding licenses of teachers who prove to be incompetent.

What Teachers Can and Should Do About Certification

Most teachers can have influence on certification standards only indirectly through conferences, publication, and policies of state and national professional associations, particularly TEPS commissions.

Chapter 9

Economic Welfare of Teachers

It is generally agreed that all occupational groups have a right to organize and to work collectively on behalf of economic welfare and desirable working conditions. It is also widely recognized that adequate economic welfare of teachers and desirable working conditions benefit the student and the public because they attract competent persons to teaching and raise the morale and teaching effectiveness of teachers in service.

Economic welfare is defined here as including (1) salaries; (2) retirement benefits; and (3) fringe benefits such as leaves of absence, health and life insurance, and income protection during disability.

Economic welfare is closely related to conditions of work and maintenance of professional organizations which will be reviewed in the following chapters, and indirectly related to all other professional problems described in previous chapters.

History of Economic Welfare of Teachers

Although economic remuneration of teachers is generally believed to be less than it should be, a review of history reveals that great gains have been made during the past century and particularly during the past few decades.

1. Salaries

Salaries of teachers may be analyzed in terms of at least four factors: (a) dollar amounts, (b) relation to earnings of other occupational groups, (c) relationships of salaries for different types of positions and persons within the teaching profession, and (d) means of determining salaries.

a. In terms of dollars, average salaries of elementary and secondary school teachers advanced from an estimated $260 in 1890, to approximately $6,500 in 1966; however much of the apparent increase is negated by the decrease in purchasing power of the dollar during that time. Exact comparisons in terms of "real" purchasing power are difficult to make for periods prior to World War I because of a paucity of comparative data on the cost of living; but there is no doubt that teachers' real incomes have increased greatly as have the incomes of almost all Americans. Since the end of World War II alone, the real incomes of teachers have more than doubled.

b. The relationship of growth in teachers' salaries to increased earnings of other occupational groups has fluctuated in a cyclical pattern over the past century.

(1) In periods of wartime inflation salaries of teachers have tended to advance at a slower rate than average earnings of other groups.

(2) In 1948, average salaries of teachers were slightly below the average earnings of all wage and salary workers, but by 1965 they were about seventeen percent above average earnings.

c. Salaries for different positions within the field of education have followed a long trend toward greater equalization. Since the beginning of this century differences between salaries of (1) men and women, (2) administrators and classroom teachers, (3) elementary, secondary, and college teachers, and (4) rural and city teachers have grown relatively smaller. The reductions in salary differentials have come about because of general socio-economic and political factors applying to most fields of work as well as to changing conditions within the teaching profession.

d. Means of determining teacher salaries have undergone three main phases of development: (1) individual bargaining between the teacher and the school system, (2) fixed salary schedules for different grade levels, and (3) the single salary schedule.

(1) Individual bargaining was common through the beginning of this century. This placed the individual teacher in a weak position because, within the confines of each public school district, there was no competing employer. It also made it easy for school boards to play favorites for political or other reasons. It was detrimental to the morale of most teachers. During the period of individual bargaining, and extending somewhat into the era of fixed salary schedules in the twenties and thirties, the beginning salary for teachers, especially in elementary schools, was frequently at a bare subsistence level.

(2) The position-type schedule, establishing a fixed salary for every school level, became common by 1920. It was based on the assumption that almost anyone could teach young children and that it is more difficult and requires greater preparation to teach more mature students.

(3) The single salary schedule began to spread steadily in the 1920's and achieved almost universal adoption by 1950. The single salary schedule bases compensation only upon the amount of preparation of a teacher and how long a teacher has taught. There is no distinction made on the basis of sex, grade level taught, or quality of teaching. Adoption of single salary schedules was stimulated by shortages of elementary teachers and the growth of scientific study of educational procedures. The latter placed increasing importance upon early child growth and development and supported the concept that while secondary school teachers need to know more about a particular subject, elementary school teachers need to know more about children and the learning process. The single salary schedule was stimulated by, and, in turn fostered, higher professional standards and increased preparation of elementary school teachers.

2. The Development of Teacher Retirement Benefits

a. Retirement systems for teachers grew out of voluntary mutual-benefit plans established by teachers in big cities beginning about 1870.

b. Beginning about 1895, city and state governmental units appropriated special funds for pension payments to retired teachers. Pension plans did not require contributions from teachers, but the amounts paid were very meager.

c. Beginning in 1917, pension plans began giving way to city and state-wide joint-contributory retirement plans in which teachers and employing bodies made regular fixed payments to retirement funds.

d. When the federal Social Security system was instituted in 1935, public employees, including teachers, were not covered by the Social Security retirement benefits. Many teacher leaders at first opposed Social Security for teachers because its application to teachers could be made only if existing retirement plans were eliminated. However, amendments to the federal law in 1950 and 1954 made it possible for teachers to be covered by both teacher retirement and Social Security. By 1963, thirty-eight states had adopted Social Security for teachers in addition to or in combination with their retirement plans.

3. Expansion of Fringe Benefits for Teachers

a. During the 1930's many teachers and other public employees enjoyed more liberal provisions for vacation and payment while on sick leave than did most other occupational groups.

b. Beginning in the 1940's, more generous leave provisions and new types of fringe benefits were widely applied in private industry. Such benefits included group health insurance, life insurance, sick pay, and subsidization of advanced study related to one's work.

c. By 1960, scores of fringe benefits not generally available to teachers were provided by many private and public employers.

d. In recent years both school systems and teacher associations have rapidly expanded fringe benefits to teachers.

Current Status of Economic Welfare of Teachers

As far as economic welfare is concerned, teachers "never had it so good." On the average, salaries, retirement benefits, and fringe benefits are at record highs. But two characteristics of prevailing economic conditions in teaching are still particularly striking. First, there are tremendous differences in salaries and the other remuneration among states and school systems; and secondly, the economic benefits to teachers are generally below those of most professions and many other fields of work requiring equivalent preparation and responsibility. Another characteristic of current economic conditions in teaching is the complexity of salary schedules, retirement plans, and fringe benefits offered by various school systems. This requires a teacher to develop understanding of the most important factors involved if he is to make a wise choice of school systems in which to work and if he is to work intelligently in improving conditions in the school system he does choose.

1. Teacher Salaries

a. In 1966, the average salary of all public elementary and secondary school teachers was about $6,500. This represented a gain of five percent over the year before, a rate of increase that is typical of annual gains over the previous decade.

b. The secondary teachers averaged about $6,800 compared to $6,300 for elementary school teachers. This difference was due primarily to the prevalence among high school teachers of higher amounts of education and greater longevity of service rather than to differences in schedules.

c. The average teacher salary in 1965-66 in the lowest paying state, Mississippi, was only about half of the average for Alaska, the highest state. The range of difference between the lowest and highest paying school districts in the country is even greater than the range of average state salaries.

d. Average salaries of the instructional staffs in colleges and universities are considerably higher than those paid to elementary or secondary school teachers. There are great differences, however, according to type of institution and professorial rank.

2. Salary Schedules

a. Almost all public school systems now publish fixed salary schedules containing at least the following information which should be studied carefully by teachers considering a position in any given school system:

(1) Beginning salary with a bachelor's degree

(2) Additional salary for advanced study or degrees

(3) Amount of annual increment of salary and how determined. In most schedules the increment is practically automatic; many require periodic evidence of professional growth to advance on the salary schedule; and some require satisfactory performance ratings. Only a small percent of all school systems provide differentiation of pay for "merit" or "superior service." A growing number of school systems are adopting "index" or "ratio" salary schedules such as are described on a following page.

(4) Number of steps to maximum of schedule. Typically this is eleven or twelve years to the top of the bachelor's degree

Table 1

Sample Teacher Salary Schedule Using Fixed Dollar Increments

STEP	B.A.	M.A.	M.A. + 30	PH.D.
1	$ 5,600	$ 6,300	$ 6,700	$ 7,200
2	5,800	6,500	6,900	7,400
3	6,000	6,700	7,100	7,600
4	6,200	6,900	7,300	7,800
5	6,500	7,250	7,700	8,200
6	6,700	7,450	7,900	8,400
7	7,000	7,750	8,200	8,700
8	7,300	8,050	8,500	9,000
9	7,500	8,350	8,800	9,300
10	7,800	8,650	9,100	9,600
11	8,100	8,950	9,400	9,900
12	8,400	9,250	9,700	10,200
13		9,550	10,000	10,500
14		9,850	10,300	10,800
15		10,150	10,600	11,100
16		10,450	10,900	11,400

schedule and at least thirteen or fourteen years to the maximums for higher degrees. In addition to the regularly scheduled maximums some school systems offer longevity increments periodically, but not annually, for long-term service. Illustrative parts of a typical salary schedule are reproduced in Table 1 on page 62.

b. Index or ratio salary schedules are being used in increasing numbers of school districts. The gist of such schedules is that all salary levels are stated in terms of ratio to a base salary, usually the first step on the bachelor's schedule, rather than in terms of dollar amounts alone. Administrators and supervisors are usually assigned index numbers also. Thus, if a school system wishes, for example, to double the salary of a teacher with a master's degree in ten years, it assigns an index number of 2.00 to the tenth step on the master's degree schedule. Different ratios are assigned for different levels of preparation as well as experience levels as indicated in the sample index schedule reproduced in Table 2 on page 64. These advantages are claimed for index schedules:

(1) Once relationships of different positions on a schedule are established, the same proportionate relationships are maintained automatically any time the base salary is changed.

(2) It encourages all educators, regardless of experience, school level, or position to work cooperatively for salary advancement, since all automatically benefit proportionately from any increase in the base salary.

(3) It simplifies the process of determining and/or bargaining for salary changes.

3. Retirement Benefits

a. Every state now has a retirement program for public school teachers. In some cases large cities have their own systems.

b. Provisions vary greatly from one system to another, but the following are representative provisions of retirement plans.

(1) Teachers contribute about five percent of salary which is automatically deducted from their pay. The state or school system contributes at least a like amount.

(2) Benefits paid to teachers upon retirement depend upon years of service and age of retirement.

Table 2

Sample Index Salary Schedule*

All salaries equal index × $5,650 base

A. TEACHERS

STEP	B.A. INDEX	B.A. AM'T.	M.A. INDEX	M.A. AM'T.	M.A. + 30 INDEX	M.A. + 30 AM'T.	PH.D. INDEX	PH.D. AM'T.
1	1.00	$ 5,650	1.15	$ 6,498	1.25	$ 7,063	1.35	$ 7,628
2	1.05	5,933	1.20	6,780	1.30	7,345	1.40	7,910
3	1.10	6,215	1.25	7,063	1.35	7,628	1.45	8,193
4	1.20	6,780	1.35	7,628	1.45	8,193	1.55	8,758
5	1.26	7,119	1.41	7,967	1.51	8,532	1.61	9,097
6	1.32	7,458	1.47	8,306	1.57	8,871	1.67	9,436
7	1.38	7,797	1.53	8,645	1.63	9,210	1.73	9,775
8	1.44	8,136	1.59	8,984	1.69	9,549	1.79	10,114
9	1.50	8,475	1.65	9,323	1.75	9,888	1.85	10,453
10	1.55	8,758	1.70	9,605	1.80	10,170	1.90	10,735
11	1.60	9,040	1.75	9,888	1.85	10,453	1.95	11,018
12	1.65	9,323	1.80	10,170	1.90	10,735	2.00	11,300
13	1.70	9,605	1.85	10,453	1.95	11,018	2.05	11,583
14	——	——	1.90	10,735	2.00	11,300	2.10	11,865
15	——	——	1.95	11,018	2.05	11,583	2.15	12,148

* Many salary schedules include provision for more preparation levels than shown here, such as B.A. + 15 hrs., M.A. + 30 hrs.

B. ADMINISTRATORS AND SUPERVISORS

GRADE STEP	A INDEX	B INDEX	C INDEX	D INDEX	E INDEX	F INDEX	G INDEX
1	1.65	1.90	2.05	2.20	2.35	2.50	2.65
2	1.70	1.95	2.10	2.25	2.40	2.60	2.80
3	1.75	2.00	2.15	2.30	2.45	2.70	2.95
4	1.80	2.05	2.20	2.35	2.50	2.80	3.10
5	1.85	2.10	2.25	2.40	2.55	2.90	3.25
6	1.90	2.15	2.30	2.45	2.60	3.00	3.35
7	2.00	2.25	2.40	2.55	2.70	3.10	3.45
8	2.10	2.35	2.50	2.65	2.80	3.20	3.55

(3) A frequent objective is to provide retirement benefits, at age sixty-five after thirty to thirty-five years of service, equal to one half of average earnings during the last, or highest, five to ten years of earnings.

(4) Except for Social Security there is practically no transfer of retirement fund credits from one state or city to another.

(5) A teacher who leaves a state or city retirement system may usually take with him all contributions he has paid into a retirement system but is not credited with the employer's contributions.

(6) Many retirement plans allow early retirement before age sixty-five but at a reduced benefit.

(7) Often the retirement plan also provides payments in case of disability before retirement and survivor's benefits in case of death.

4. Fringe Benefits Provided by School Systems

a. *Sick Leave.* Almost every school system provides sick leave with full pay. The median number of days provided annually is ten. Ninety days is the median number of days which can be accumulated in school systems with student enrollments of 12,000 or more.

b. *Personal Leave.* Increasing numbers of school systems provide a few days a year of leave with pay for urgent personal reasons such as sickness or death in the immediate family, religious holidays, jury duty, and court summonses.

c. *Sabbatical Leave.* This type of leave for study, travel, or recuperation of health, although common in higher education, is offered in only a small number of school systems. Typical payment during sabbatical leave is one-half salary.

d. *Insurance.* Many school systems and teacher organizations offer one or more of the following types of insurance either completely paid for, partially paid for, or at group rates paid for by the individual teacher.

(1) Group health insurance, including hospitalization, surgical, medical, and major medical.

(2) Group life insurance, usually term insurance.

(3) Liability insurance, to cover possible liability arising from student injuries due to alleged negligence of a teacher.

e. *Tax-Sheltered Annuity.* This costs the school system nothing except expenses of administration, but it yields teachers legitimate tax savings. Under such a plan a teacher may authorize a school system to reduce his annual salary and apply the amount of the reduction toward the purchase of an annuity payable upon retirement. The amount of such payment is exempt from federal income tax until it is received upon retirement.

f. Other fringe benefits offered by some school systems include *Maternity Leave, Professional Leave* (to attend conferences or other professional activities), *Health Services,* and *Tuition Reimbursement.*

Problems and Issues in Teacher Welfare

1. Merit Pay

Merit pay is one of the most controversial and long-standing issues in relation to economic welfare of teachers. To many school-board members and citizens and to some educators it seems logical, fair, and advantageous to pay the more effective teachers more money.

Merit pay has been tried over a number of years in many school systems, but each year about as many school systems drop merit pay plans as start them. Why has merit pay failed to work in practice? There are a number of reasons, the most significant of which are listed here.

a. No generally acceptable way has been found to identify or evaluate outstanding teaching in an objective way.

b. Merit pay has hurt the morale of teachers, sometimes even those receiving the extra pay.

c. Some school boards have used merit pay as a means of keeping regular salary schedules low.

d. Some merit pay plans may actually harm the instructional program by causing teachers to seek to please the evaluators through means which may not be best for the instructional program.

2. The Depressing Effect of Women Teachers on Salaries

Even though equal pay for women and men is accepted public policy, it is still true that women's earnings in general are far lower than those of men. Many women would find it difficult to earn more than they can in teaching, while many men could follow more lucrative careers. Furthermore, many married women use their earnings to supplement their husband's income while most men generally depend upon their earnings to support a family. This is one reason that there are just about twice as many women as men in the public schools. But state and national equal opportunity laws, changing social attitudes in favor of "career women," and other trends discussed in "The Outlook for Economic Welfare of Teachers" section of this chapter, promise to alleviate this problem.

3. Uneven Supply and Demand in Various Teaching Fields

The prevailing single salary schedule pays all teachers alike regardless of great differences in the competition from related fields. For example, high school science and math teachers have been lured away from teaching by high salaries in industry and government for which they may qualify, while English or social studies teachers are much less likely to find greater economic rewards outside of teaching. Hence, good science and math teachers have been much scarcer in our schools than some other kinds of teachers, or they have made relatively greater sacrifices to stay in teaching. To alleviate this type of problem it has been suggested that salary schedules be adjusted to pay more to teachers in fields of short supply. To date this idea has gained little acceptance in practice, but the problem of uneven supply of different kinds of teachers persist.

4. Concept of Teaching as Part-Time Work

The long summer vacation and seemingly short school day tend to make many citizens and officials regard teaching to be less than a full-time occupation and hence deserving of less than full-time pay. Actually, many teachers devote much of their vacation period to study at their own expense, but about fifteen percent of women teachers and over seventy percent of men teachers work part-time outside teaching, either summers or during the school year.

Even though many teachers may leave school at about 3 P.M., correcting papers, preparation of teaching plans and materials, and other related work brings the average work week for elementary school teachers to 48½ hours and for high school teachers to 46 hours. Therefore, on the average, teachers probably work as many hours during a year as many people who work 40 hours or less with shorter vacations. But the averages obscure great individual differences. A survey by the NEA Research Division found that 11.4 percent of all public school teachers reported working 60 or more hours a week at teaching duties, while 11.2 percent worked less than 35 hours a week.[1] Solutions to these conditions range between the two extremes outlined here.

a. Pay all teachers enough to enable them to devote all of their time to teaching and recognize the summer vacation as necessary to refresh teachers' energies and to extend and bring up to date professional knowledge and skills.

b. Provide optional opportunities for some teachers to work on a twelve-month basis, with four weeks of vacation, at a higher rate of pay than those who don't choose to work during the summer.

5. Lack of Reciprocity of Retirement Plans

One of the major problems facing career public school teachers is the fact that accumulated equities in retirement systems cannot be transferred from one state to another. Thus a teacher who works in one state for any considerable period of time finds himself "locked in." If he leaves the state in which he is teaching he may withdraw his own contributions, usually with interest, but he loses all rights to the contributions the state or city has paid to the retirement fund. He faces serious economic loss if he has to start all over again in building retirement benefits in another state. Some states alleviate this problem by allowing what is called "vesting." Under this plan the teacher is vested with rights to an annuity at retirement based on the state contribution as well as his own if he leaves his money in the retirement fund. This is called a "deferred benefit."

Many college teachers do enjoy transferability of their retirement funds from one institution to another through a national nongovernmental plan called Teachers Annuity and Insurance Association.

---

[1] National Education Association, Research Division, *The American Public-School Teacher, 1960-61.* (Washington, D. C.: the Association, 1963), pp. 54-55.

The Outlook for Economic Welfare of Teachers

1. Higher Salaries

If teacher salaries continue to increase at the same rate they have in the decade prior to 1966, average salaries for classroom teachers will approach $10,000 by 1975. However, there is increasing sentiment in favor of making salary increases more selective as outlined below.

2. Differentiated Salaries

It is unlikely that there will be any widespread adoption of pay plans rewarding teachers directly for merit, but somewhat the same effect of differentiated salaries is likely to be established through wide application of the following policies which now exist in some school systems:

a. Proportionately greater differentials in pay for advanced study or evidence of professional growth by long-term career teachers

b. Twelve-month contracts with extra pay for teaching in summer school, revising curriculums, or other professional work during the summer

c. Extra pay for extra duties such as supervision of student teachers, demonstration teaching, and major extra-curricular activities

d. Higher pay for leaders of teaching "teams"

e. Higher pay for teacher specialists who develop special skills such as in teaching remedial reading.

3. Decreasing Difference Between Salaries of Teachers and Administrators

The present relationship between basic salaries of teachers and administrators is likely to be maintained through application of index salary schedules, but there is likely to be greater opportunity for limited numbers of career teachers to approach administrative salaries by earning extra pay as outlined here.

4. Reciprocity of Retirement Provisions

As the mobility of Americans increases there is likely to be increasing pressure from teachers for transferability of retirement credits. It is possible that some national retirement system will be established similar in nature to the "portable" TIAI plan now available in higher education.

5. Extension of Fringe Benefits Directly Available Through Professional Associations

It seems likely that as teachers acquire disposable income above that needed for immediate necessities of life they will seek additional fringe benefits from their professional associations on both a voluntary contributory basis and automatically as a benefit of membership. Such benefits will include many types of low-rate group insurance, tax-sheltered annuities, and mutual investment funds. Although many state-sponsored plans will continue, lower costs for larger group programs will probably stimulate greatest expansion of such benefits at the national level.

6. Expansion of Negotiation by Teacher Organizations on Behalf of Members

The spread of formal negotiation procedures between school boards and teacher organizations on behalf of their members, or all teachers in a school system, is likely to result in improved economic welfare of teachers.

What Teachers Can and Should Do About Their Economic Welfare

1. Selection of School System and Welfare Options

The most immediate way in which a teacher can affect his own economic welfare is to make a careful choice of school system in which to seek employment. Economic factors alone should not be the sole criteria, but they are important enough to merit more than casual study. Prospective teachers and teachers considering a change in position often give primary consideration to the beginning or the average salary in a given school system; but the structure of the salary schedule, the nature of the retirement plan, and fringe benefits available from the school system and/or professional organizations are worth consideration in light of the conditions described on previous pages.

2. Participation in Professional Group Action

As an individual the teacher is virtually powerless to advance economic rewards of teaching in a school system. But in organized groups teachers can achieve considerable advancement in economic welfare as well as other aspects of education. In order to determine how teachers can be most effective in working for economic welfare and desirable conditions of work, it is necessary to understand the principal factors that affect welfare and the working climate. This writer has identified eight such factors: (1) teacher supply and demand, (2) competition among school systems and with other fields of work, (3) administrative initiative, (4) public opinion, (5) bases of economic support, (6) political action, (7) collective negotiation, and (8) withholding of services.

The following brief analyses of each of the eight factors reveal implications for roles of teachers.

Factors Affecting Economic Welfare and Conditions of Work

1. Teacher Supply and Demand

a. One of the basic principles of our economic system is that a short supply of personnel in any field will push up the "price" of such personnel. Generally, occupations which require extensive preparation or high qualifications command high economic benefits because relatively few people are able to constitute the supply for this economic group.

b. Presumably, the rapid extension of public education to more people for longer periods of time during the past century has created an almost constant shortage of teachers. However, when the term "shortage of teachers" is used, it generally means "qualified" or "competent" teachers. From the economic standpoint there has rarely been a shortage of teachers. Either standards for admission to teaching have been so low as to make available an almost unlimited supply of potential teachers, or those responsible for employment of teachers have been allowed to waive requirements or standards on an "emergency" basis. As long as there is no real limit on supply it is difficult for any occupational group to rise above low levels of pay.

2. Competition Among School Systems and with Other Fields of Work

a. Since teachers are a rather mobile occupational group, competition among school systems and among states for the best teachers serves to push up salaries and other financial rewards. Such action is stimulated by the provision of up-to-date facts regarding salary schedules, retirement benefits, and fringe benefits. The collection and dissemination of such facts has been done by the National Education Association since 1905 and by some state teachers associations at least as long.

b. In recent years, in addition to facts about salaries in states and individual school systems, the NEA has compiled and widely distributed comparisons of earnings of teachers with other occupational groups. The findings have been used to justify higher salaries for teachers.

3. Administrative Initiative

Administrative initiative in advancing teacher welfare is closely related to the factor of competition. School boards and administrators also tend to seek to advance teacher welfare in order to maintain high teacher morale and therefore a high quality of instruction. Different assumptions regarding the importance of this factor constitute one of the important points of difference between the American Federation of Teachers and the National Education Association. Writings and speeches of representatives of the AFT tend to point up conflicts of interest between teachers and administrators while representatives of the NEA and affiliates tend to emphasize the common interests of teachers, administrators, and school boards in maintaining adequate teacher welfare.

4. Public Opinion

a. Since the public schools are supported by public funds, there is no doubt that public opinion regarding school programs and teachers is a major factor in determining teacher welfare. There are many means of influencing public opinion, but there is general agreement with the contention of the National School Public Relations Association that public relations "starts in the classroom." In a publication bearing the title *It Starts in the Classroom,* the importance of the role of the classroom teacher in shaping public opinion is described as follows:

> Because of their preparation and contacts, classroom teachers have a strategic role in interpreting the schools to the people. They are familiar with the history, philosophy, purposes, and methods of education. They are informed about psychology, child nature, and social processes. These talents can and have been used to develop the public relations programs of school systems in many communities.
>
> Good schools must have good public relations. One doesn't have to look far to see the proof. In a community where the people understand the school program and have faith in the staff the quality of education is usually high. There the classroom teachers have essential instructional materials, salaries and working conditions reach professional levels, and the educational opportunities of pupils are outstanding. Where schools are *not* good the cause may often be found in the indifference, misinformation, and distrust among the people. Public education is not likely to be better than the public's understanding of the schools.[2]

b. The above statement supports the concept that all aspects of professional group responsibility are interwoven and are related closely to the individual responsibility of being an effective teacher.

5. Base of Economic Support

a. The amount of money available for the economic welfare of public-school teachers is limited by the tax sources which provide school support. In 1962-63, according to estimates by the NEA Research Division, 57 percent of school support for the nation as a whole came from local sources, primarily real estate taxes; 39.4

[2] National School Public Relations Association, *It Starts in the Classroom: A Public Relations Handbook for Classroom Teachers* (Washington, D. C.: the Association, a department of the National Education Association, 1951), pp. 5-6.

percent came from state sources; and the remainder, only 3.6 percent, from the federal government. By 1965-66, the federal share had risen to 7.8 percent, reducing the proportion of state support to 39.1 percent, but leaving the major share, 53.1 percent to be borne by local tax sources.

b. Much has been written about the inadequacy of the real estate tax in today's world—its inflexibility, its inadequate relationship to real income, its political ramifications—and about the need for broadening the base of economic support by tapping income and consumer taxes which are collected primarily by the state and federal governments. Some states have, proportionately to population, four to five times as much taxable wealth as other states. Some school districts have several hundred times as much taxable wealth per person as others. Many finance experts have concluded that broadening the tax base for support of education through increased state and substantial federal support of education is necessary to provide adequate funds for education.

6. Political Action

a. Since it is a public enterprise, almost all aspects of public education are affected by political action, but until recently political scientists and educators have failed to give adequate attention to political aspects of education.

b. The nation's two million teachers have great potential for political action. Surveys have revealed that teachers do far better than the typical American in fulfilling their most basic responsibility in politics, exercising the vote. The NEA Research Division has reported that in the 1960 presidential election more than 90 percent of the nation's teachers voted as compared with 63.8 percent of the total population of voting age. But only 6.6 percent of teachers were active members of a political party.

c. The political effectiveness of teachers as a group has been judged, generally, to be greatest at the state level. For many years most state education associations have spearheaded legislation that has increased financial support for public schools, created larger and more effective administrative school units, advanced equalization of educational opportunity, and improved teacher salaries, tenure, and provisions for retirement.

d. At the national level the NEA has worked actively since the 1930's to extend federal financial support for education and to seek other legislation affecting education and teachers. Minor gains were made after 1917, but until the 1960's the view that education is a state and local responsibility blocked any major general aid to education. By 1965, the climate of public opinion and national politics was ripe for enactment of major financial aid to elementary and secondary schools as well as higher education. In seeking such legislation, thousands of teachers worked through their local and state associations and as individuals to influence the congressmen from their states. Such activity is destined to continue.

e. Political action of teachers at the local level has ranged from very effective to negatively effective, the latter caused in part by political naïveté of some teachers and local teacher leaders. Greater political sophistication of teachers and expertise of organization leaders is necessary.

7. Collective Negotiation

a. Much attention has been given since the beginning of the sixties to the competing efforts of the National Education Association to establish formal "professional negotiation" procedures and the efforts of the American Federation of Teachers to institute "collective bargaining." Much of the welfare-related activity of classroom teachers and their professional organizations during the foreseeable future promises to revolve, first, around choosing or rejecting a form of collective negotiation and, second, around implementing negotiation procedures, if adopted.

b. In many school systems throughout the country informal types of collective negotiation have been practiced for many years. In such school systems, representatives of local teacher organizations worked out mutually agreeable programs with the superintendent and the board of education. However, the lack of formal or binding arrangements made the effectiveness or even existence of such procedures dependent upon the vagaries of changing personalities involved. Furthermore, when the "chips were down" and mutual agreement could not be reached there was no machinery for resolving impasses.

c. Collective bargaining has been advocated by the AFT since 1938. "Professional group action" regarding teacher salaries, already practiced by many NEA-affiliated locals, was endorsed by the NEA Executive Committee in 1947. A 1963 resolution of the NEA Representative Assembly relates "professional negotiation" to "other conditions of professional service" as well as to salary.

d. An analysis of NEA and AFT statements regarding "professional negotiation" and "collective bargaining" reveals objectives which seem similar—the improvement of education and the advancement of the welfare of teachers. Even some of the procedures proposed or practiced are similar; but there are a few significant differences:

(1) The AFT collective bargaining procedures are modelled upon conventional labor union procedures, with the underlying assumption of conflict of interest between labor and "management" and the use of labor channels such as state labor boards to handle elections, grievances, and mediation.

(2) NEA advocates of professional negotiation propose special education channels to handle elections, grievances, and mediation; and they place greater emphasis upon cooperative effort and mutual agreement.

e. In practice there are many variations in negotiation procedures in the various states. This is due to differences in state laws, patterns of school organization, the nature and history of the teacher associations involved, and other factors.

8. Withholding of Services

Withholding of services has long been used as a means of achieving objectives of occupational groups. In teaching this has been done in at least four major ways: (a) partial withholding of services not required by contract; (b) concerted agreement not to renew contracts; (c) strikes; and (d) professional sanctions.

a. *Partial Withholding of Services.* A number of local associations have fostered agreement among teachers to refrain from voluntary work on extra-curricular activities. Such procedures have usually met with success only if coupled with other activities to arouse public opinion in favor of improving conditions. One important problem in applying this procedure is the lack of definition in most school systems of the precise duties required of teachers.

b. *Failure to Renew Contracts.* Some local associations have won concessions from school boards by agreement of members, well in advance of required dates for renewal of contract or notice of resignation, to refuse employment for the next school year unless stipulated conditions are met. This has often been effective and is generally considered to be ethical provided no contractual obligations are violated.

c. *Strikes.* Strikes in education, even when otherwise labelled, may be defined as concerted and complete withholding of services during a contractural period of service. Arguments offered for and against teacher strikes may be found in the section of this book on problems and issues in professional organizations. The American Federation of Teachers began to directly encourage strikes in the early 1960's. The National Education Association discourages teacher strikes and advocates use of professional sanctions instead to alleviate untenable conditions. However, NEA affiliates as well as AFT affiliates have resorted to strikes under extreme circumstances.

d. *Professional Sanctions.*

(1) The term sanctions generally refers to public censure of many kinds. It may be applied to individual members of the profession for unethical conduct or it may be applied to an entire school system.

(2) In 1963, the NEA issued *Guidelines for Professional Sanctions* in which conditions and procedures are proposed for local, state, and/or national sanctions. Sanctions are advocated only where other means of recourse have failed and then in graduated sequence ranging from (a) a public announcement of unsatisfactory conditions to (b) warnings to teachers outside the sanctioned school system that acceptance of employment in that school system will be considered to be unethical and (c) advice to teachers already in the system that they should seek employment elsewhere.

(3) One of the major effects of sanctions is to arouse public interest in improving the schools. Since this may require political action to be implemented, the achievement of objectives sought through sanctions may take months or years to realize but, for the same reason, they should usually result in long-term, rather than temporary, improvements.

Chapter 10

Work Climate

The maintenance of a desirable work climate seems to be of greater concern to teachers than any other aspect of their welfare except salaries. Satisfactory working conditions benefit students and society as well as the teacher because they have great influence on the quality of teaching that will take place. Work climate is defined here to include (1) professional status for teachers; (2) personnel policies, including procedures for resolving grievances; (3) work load, including class size; (4) instructional materials and equipment; (5) physical conditions; (6) security of position, including tenure and continuing contracts; (7) academic freedom; and (8) personal freedom.

The achievement of a desirable working climate for teaching depends, first, upon the enactment of desirable policies and second, upon effective implementation and enforcement of such provisions. There seems to be increasing recognition that although administrative leadership is important in establishing and maintaining a desirable working climate, teaching effectiveness and morale are enhanced when classroom teachers are involved to a significant degree in cooperative policy determination. Much of the activity of teacher organizations is devoted to attempts to improve conditions of work.

History and Current Status of Teaching Conditions

A comprehensive history of conditions of work for teachers in the United States would involve much of the history of education as a whole and would be complicated by great variations among different states and school systems. Therefore relatively few historical highlights of national significance are outlined below.

1. Professional Status

a. Recognition of professional status of teachers results in greater teacher freedom to make decisions on their own as well as to participate in making policies for a school or school system. The development of various aspects of professionalism is related in each of the chapters of this book.

b. Two national professional agencies previously mentioned have had particular influence in progress toward full professional status for teachers: the NEA National Commission for Teacher Education and Professional Standards, founded in 1946, and the NEA National Commission on Professional Rights and Responsibilities, founded in 1941 under the name National Commission for the Defense of Democracy Through Education. Many of the state and local counterparts of these commissions have been among the most active of professional association agencies.

2. Personnel Policies

a. In the past, the absence of clearly defined personnel policies has been a major cause of uneasiness, inefficiency, and low morale among teachers in some school systems. For a number of years the NEA and other professional organizations have urged the development by school boards in consultation with teachers, of clearly written personnel policies stating procedures for selection of teachers, duties and responsibilities of school personnel, employment conditions, teaching conditions, pupil administration, and public information. Many school systems now have such written policies readily available to teachers.

b. In 1963, the NEA Commission on Professional Rights and Responsibilities, in *Practical Personnel Policies for Good Schools,* listed the following desirable personnel policies:

Written rules to provide the basis for discussion and understanding. These rules may be in contracts or in booklets—but every teacher should have a copy.

Salary schedules, written and drafted in accordance with acceptable standards. Many issues can be settled by a salary plan worked out cooperatively.

Communication channels for clearing staff problems. Confidence is promoted by properly kept records and by prompt answers to teachers' questions.

Standards to guide transfers, promotions, and assignments. When agreed upon by all concerned they are likely to follow reasonable and ethical patterns.

Classroom conditions suitable for good instruction. Adequate lighting, reasonable class size, and freedom from unnecessary interruptions are among the conditions requisite to teaching success.

Instructional supplies available in adequate amount and with consideration of the experiences to be given to pupils. More effective use will be made of materials if teachers help select or develop them.

Bulletins and outlines of the program of study for both experienced and new teachers. Such guideposts to instruction are helpful also to pupils, parents, and the general public.

Pupil evaluation procedures which are clearly defined. For the best interest of all concerned, methods of evaluation of pupil progress should be mutually understood in the community by parents, teachers and pupils.

Parent contacts with the classroom teacher for the guidance of children. Worthwhile conferences requiring planning and sufficient time can be arranged best when classroom teachers, administrators, and parents work together.[1]

---

[1] National Education Association, Commission on Professional Rights and Responsibilities, *Practical Personnel Policies for Good Schools* (Washington, D.C.: the Commission, 1963), pp. 4-5.

c. Until the 1950's, hardly any school systems included in their personnel policies a formal procedure for handling grievances of school personnel. A "grievance" in personnel relations is a complaint of alleged unjust treatment, in the opinion of an employee, that fails to receive adequate or just consideration through normal administrative channels. Increasing numbers of school systems are adopting formal grievance machinery including provision at the last step for arbitration by a panel of persons chosen by or acceptable to the employee and the employer. Grievance procedures are often spelled out in negotiated agreements between school boards and local teacher organizations. In a few cases grievance procedures are required by state law or regulation.

3. Work Load and Class Size

a. As reported in the preceding chapter on Economic Welfare, the average number of hours teachers worked per week in 1960-61 was close to 48. This was about the same as a decade earlier. Since 1960, much has been done in some school systems to reduce excessive work loads and to allow fuller utilization of the professional skills of teachers. These measues have included the following:

(1) Reduction of average class size

(2) Increased clerical assistance for teachers

(3) Use of data processing equipment for records, reports, and scheduling

(4) Employment of nonprofessional assistants to perform non-instructional duties such as lunchroom supervision

(5) Employment of teacher assistants to work under the supervision of a fully qualified teacher

(6) Employment of technicians for services such as audio-visual aids

(7) Team teaching, combining the above procedures, with teacher specialization and variations in class size for different purposes.

b. Some of the major influences in reducing teacher load, making more effective use of teachers' instructional skills, and improving other conditions of work during the ten year period before 1966 are listed in the following points. More complete information on the reports mentioned may be found in the Bibliography.

(1) Private foundations have sponsored a number of experimental and demonstration projects designed to make maximum effective use of teachers' time. One of the most publicized projects related to conditions of work in the high school, financed in great part by the Fund for the Advancement of Education and the Ford Foundation, was a project of the National Association of Secondary-School Principals bearing the lengthy title Commission on the Experimental Study of the Utilization of the Staff in the Secondary School. The recommendations of the Commission were published in 1961 in *Focus on Change: Guide to Better Schools.* The recommendations of the Commission have commonly been referred to as the "Trump Plan," after the name of the staff director of the Commission, J. Lloyd Trump.

(2) The NEA Department of Classroom Teachers' sponsored Conditions of Work Project identified the problems as listed on previous pages, and suggested policies and principles related to these problems. In addition to disseminating this information through publications such as *Conditions of Work for Quality Teaching,* the Department sponsored workshops and other programs to stimulate and aid state and local associations to improve teaching conditions.

(3) A three-year study of the NEA Project on Instruction made recommendations on teaching conditions in its final report, *Schools for the Sixties,* published in 1963, and in greater detail in *Planning and Organizing for Teaching.* The work of the Project has been continued and extended by the NEA Center for the Study of Instruction established in 1963.

(4) From 1964 to 1966, the Department of Classroom Teachers' sponsored Time To Teach Project. This project helped conduct experimental projects in a number of schools around the country in which entire school staffs participated in development and application of plans to lighten unnecessary burdens of teachers and to make best use of teachers' time. Much of the theoretical background of the Project is to be found in *Innovations for Time to Teach* and a detailed summary of the experimental programs is in the *Time to Teach Action Report.*

(5) In addition to the broad activities listed above, many special interest departments of the NEA and independent organi-

zations such as the National Council on English have conducted studies and made recommendations regarding teacher load and other conditions of work.

(6) The American Federation has devoted a large proportion of its total program to conditions of work. An analysis of the 1963 resolutions of the AFT made by this writer revealed that more resolutions were presented on conditions of work than on all other topics combined.

4. Instructional Materials and Equipment

a. Inadequate instructional materials and equipment have long been a serious problem in many schools. Efforts to improve teachers' salaries have indirectly helped to create shortages of materials and equipment because there has been a tendency in many school systems to apply most new funds to teacher salaries, leaving insufficient money for books and other instructional materials. On the average, seventy percent of a school system's operating budget is devoted to professional staff salaries and thirty percent to instructional materials, maintenance, and other supporting services.

b. The enactment of the federal National Defense Education Act in 1958 and the Elementary and Secondary Education Act in 1965 provided millions of dollars specifically earmarked for books, instructional materials, and equipment. These funds have enabled some school systems to approach the goal of adequate instructional aids for the first time in their histories.

5. Physical Conditions

a. During World War II a tremendous backlog of needed school buildings was created. Soaring school enrollments after the war increased the shortage of buildings further; but by 1965, school systems seemed to be slowly catching up to needs. Nevertheless, millions of children and thousands of teachers still work in old school buildings that are not conducive to good learning, are damaging to health and morale, and in some cases are dangerous firetraps. Unfortunately, many of the worst physical conditions are in slum areas in the big cities and in poor rural areas. It is in those very areas that good facilities are especially needed to give students and teachers the special lift they need for educational success in the face of other difficulties.

b. By 1966, the greatest relative shortage of educational facilities seemed to be developing at the college level. This was due to a combination of great increases in the number of college-age youth and in the proportion of such youth seeking to enter college.

6. Security of Position

The right of a teacher to maintain his position as long as he renders satisfactory service is commonly called "tenure." Tenure is usually given after a period of successful probationary experience of two to three years. Dismissal of a teacher protected by tenure can be done only for gross misconduct or inefficiency as defined by law, regulation, or contract. Tenure laws usually provide for an official hearing and appeals procedure. Such job security was generally not provided prior to 1920 and is still not enjoyed by all teachers in the United States.

a. In 1919, the NEA established a Committee on Tenure and Academic Freedom. One of the activities of this committee has been to work for the adoption of tenure legislation in all states. In 1920, only five states had provided by law for job security of teachers.

b. By 1966, approximately forty states provided tenure either on a state-wide basis or in some of the school systems in the state. Between fifteen and thirty percent of all public school teachers in the United States are not covered by tenure laws, depending on one's exact definition of tenure. Some states or school systems which do not have tenure laws do provide a continuing contract arrangement. Under a continuing contract a teacher remains in his position indefinitely unless notified by a specified day of the year that his contract will not be renewed after the close of the school year.

c. In 1961, the NEA Tenure Committee was merged with the Defense Commission to form the Professional Rights and Responsibilities Commission. This Commission and its state and local counterparts provide counsel, and, when necessary, legal aid to teachers who have been unjustly treated.

d. In 1949, the NEA established the DuShane Defense Fund to be used to assist in the correction of any injustice which, if uncontested, might have serious implications for the profession. In 1965, alarmed by the prospect that many teachers might lose their positions because of integration of schools or other factors which threatened great turmoil in education, the NEA initiated action to raise a "Million Dollar Fund for Teacher Rights." This Fund, like the DuShane Defense Fund and the activities of the Professional Rights and Responsibilities Commission, applies to academic freedom and personal freedom as well as to protection of tenure. The Fund was supported by individual contributions by teachers and group contributions of state and local associations.

7. Academic Freedom

Academic freedom may be defined most simply as the right of teachers to teach the truth as they see it. Academic freedom is closely related to security of position and to personal freedom.

a. The tradition of academic freedom is greater in higher education than in public elementary and secondary schools. But even in colleges and universities in the United States there was a relative lack of academic freedom until about the middle of the 19th century. Prior to that period there was strong domination of the content of college teaching imposed by religious sponsorship or influence in institutions of higher education. The struggle of college teachers to obtain or advance academic freedom continues to be a major interest of organizations of college professors, especially of the American Association of University Professors (AAUP).

b. Teachers in elementary and secondary schools have had their freedom to teach restricted in at least three ways: (1) through laws enacted by state legislatures and regulation by lay school boards of education, (2) by administrative and supervisory regulation, and (3) by pressures from individuals or groups of the general public. These pressures have often prevented elementary and secondary school teachers from dealing adequately with controversial subjects such as the United Nations, different political and economic systems, and scientific teachings that may seem to conflict with religious beliefs, such as the theory of evolution. As teachers have gained increased amounts of education and assumed initiative for determining methods and content of education, the degree of academic freedom allowed them has slowly increased.

8. Personal Freedom

Personal freedom should not be confused with academic freedom. Academic freedom relates to what the teacher does in the school in connection with the teaching process. Personal freedom relates to the right of teachers to engage in activities outside the school on the same basis as other citizens. In this regard, as in academic freedom, college teachers have enjoyed a much higher degree of personal freedom than elementary and secondary school teachers. Restrictions have been imposed upon such personal matters as drinking, smoking, dating, and political activities of teachers. Such restrictions have been justified by the belief that the teacher's behavior influences youth by example, even outside the school. However, individual teachers and teacher organizations have resisted the imposition of the double standard which prevents teachers from enjoying the same personal liberties as other respectable citizens.

a. Generally, teachers have enjoyed more personal freedom in the large urban areas than in rural areas or small towns. This is due partly to the fact that in large cities teachers have been "lost in the crowd."

b. By the mid-1960's, most communities did allow teachers almost as much personal freedom as the general population. However, the right of teachers to express attitudes or beliefs in relation to economic, political, and social affairs is still a highly controversial issue in some communities.

c. Political activities of teachers and their organizations may be divided into two basic types: (1) political action relating to society in general, and (2) political activity related to the improvement of education.

d. The major national agency working toward acceptance by teachers and the public of active participation of educators in the making of public policy has been the Citizenship Committee of the NEA. This committee was founded in 1939. In 1964, it was enlarged and began to increase its influence through policy statements, conferences, and publications.

Problems and Issues Relating to Teaching Conditions

1. Lack of Teacher Autonomy

One of the main causes for dissatisfaction of some teachers is the relative lack of freedom to decide how to teach and what to teach.

a. One extreme viewpoint relative to this problem holds that all major decisions regarding the curriculum, school organization, methods of teaching, and selection of instructional materials should be made by administrative and supervisory personnel, presumably because they have superior knowledge of these matters and because there needs to be a high degree to articulation of curriculum and methods so that students will be assured of continuous development from one grade to another.

b. At the other extreme is the view that, as a professional person, the classroom teacher should have a wide range of choice of methods, content, and materials to be used in his own teaching.

c. Another view supports involvement of classroom teachers in group planning of major curriculum, school organization, and other arrangements for effective teaching, but with opportunity for individual classroom teachers to shape many aspects of their teaching within the broad framework of school policies.

2. Excessive Bureaucracy in School Administration

In many school systems, particularly in some larger cities, the effectiveness of teachers is severely handicapped by cumbersome, slow-moving, and, in some cases, autocratic or inefficient administration. Even in large school systems that are fairly well-supported financially, there is often a great time lag between recognition of needs of teachers and students and the provision of appropriate supporting services and instructional materials.

3. Lack of Adequate Machinery for Handling Grievances

In some school systems the lack of a clearly defined grievance procedure causes many teachers to build up bitter resentment, frustration, and negative attitudes toward the school administration. Formal written grievance procedures, it has been found, can improve morale of teachers and can protect administrators as well as teachers from unfair treatment or charges.

4. Misassignment of Teachers

Administrative practices in a number of school systems adversely affect the quality of instruction by placing teachers in situations for which they lack competence.

a. The most common type of misassignment is placement in a subject field or grade level for which the teacher is not adequately prepared. This is done as an administrative or economic expedient to balance schedules, or to provide broader programs in small schools which cannot employ a full-time teacher for every subject offered.

b. In large cities another type of misassignment places teachers into positions and schools in underprivileged neighborhoods posing problems with which many teachers cannot cope. Such problems are created by the following factors.

(1) The rapid influx of underprivileged Negroes and other minority groups in the large cities pose difficult challenges to teachers. Many of these people come from poverty-stricken, rural areas and are not well adjusted to urban living, academic learning, or middle class values and modes of behavior.

(2) Some city systems, through formal or informal procedures, assign teachers with the greatest amount of seniority to the easiest teaching assignments. New teachers are often assigned to the most difficult schools or the largest classes. Many such new teachers do not survive this baptism of fire. They either leave the profession or develop negative attitudes toward teaching.

(3) Most teachers receive little preparation in college for the real world of the schools in slum areas. Often they do their observation and student teaching in campus demonstration schools or wealthy suburban schools in which classes are small and children are highly motivated to learn. Then they find they cannot find a position in such a school after graduation from college.

5. Excessive Work Load

a. Excessive work loads may be caused by one or more of the following conditions:

(1) Too long a period of continuous teaching. In the elementary schools particularly some teachers have not had an opportunity to be duty-free even during lunch nor have they had enough time to plan or prepare for their instructional duties.

(2) Nonprofessional tasks required of teachers. Teachers are generally required to do a large amount of clerical work, record keeping, and even housekeeping duties, which could be done by nonprofessional personnel.

(3) Excessively large classes. For a long time educators have expressed the opinion that the number of pupils in a class should not exceed twenty-five. However, research has revealed little conclusive evidence regarding the effect of class size on learning. Studies show that many factors affect optimum class size. Currently many school systems are trying combinations of large classes, small classes, and individual study for various purposes.

b. In 1959, the Educational Policies Commission advocated a minimum of twenty professional personnel for every 1,000 students in a school system. This takes into account the various specialists and administrative staff as well as classroom teachers. At the time only relatively few privileged school districts met this criterion.

6. Extracurricular Duties

a. This is a problem which exists primarily in high schools. Extracurricular duties are often distributed very unequally, with the most talented, able, and willing teachers drawing heavy loads, while some teachers provide little or no such service. One attempted means of solving this problem has been the provision of extra pay for extra-curricular duties. This, in turn, has created at least two problems.

(1) First, there is difficulty in providing comparable compensation for different kinds of activities.

(2) Secondly, the extra pay may increase the welfare and morale of a teacher, but it will not prevent him from becoming less effective in his regular teaching because of a heavy load.

b. Another solution is to include extracurricular activities as part of the regular school day or as part of the regular teacher load. Thus a teacher who provides extracurricular supervision or instruction is relieved of some of his regular teaching assignments.

7. Lack of Adequate Supporting Services

In order to take full advantage of modern developments in specialized fields related to education, a school system needs to provide assistance to the teacher from personnel such as guidance specialists, psychologists, librarians, audiovisual technicians, remedial reading experts, and, in the elementary school, various subject area specialists. In many school systems only a token attempt at providing such services is made, with the result that neither teachers nor students benefit.

8. Lack of Security of Position in Some School Systems

In 1966, approximately fifteen percent of all public school teachers had practically no security of position. In states where such protection is lacking there have been charges that teachers have been dismissed for reasons not directly related to the performance of their professional duties, such as politics or controversy over racial integration.

The Outlook for Teaching Conditions

The outlook for improvement of teaching conditions is very favorable, stimulated in part by national legislation passed in the mid-1960's.

1. Additional Staff and Services for Underprivileged Students

a. Class size of schools in underprivileged areas will be greatly reduced so that students needing the most help can get individual attention.

b. Early childhood education such as that supported by the federal Head Start programs initiated in 1965 will prepare underprivileged students for formal education.

c. Remedial specialists, librarians, teacher aides, adequate instructional materials, and equipment will help classroom teachers to achieve a higher degree of success in teaching.

d. Many colleges and universities that prepare teachers will institute special theoretical and practical training for teachers who plan to enter, or are already in, schools enrolling large numbers of disadvantaged students.

2. Improved Libraries and Instructional Materials

Additional federal as well as state and local funds will provide teachers with the tools they need to carry out a successful instructional program.

3. Innovations in Education

a. Innovations in school organization such as team teaching and the use of technical and other nonprofessional teacher aides may ease the strain on teachers while improving the instructional program.

b. Expanded support of educational research may bring more efficient and effective means of instruction.

4. Democratization of School Administration

Teachers will have considerable voice in determining the conditions under which they work.

a. In many cases administrators voluntarily involve teachers in determining school policies because of the teacher's firsthand knowledge of the school situation and because it has been found that people usually work more enthusiastically and effectively when they share in determining policies regarding their work. Much of such policymaking will take place in individual schools under the leadership of the principal.

b. More aggressive and powerful teacher organizations will continue to press for school improvements of all kinds. In the historically significant actions in Utah in 1964 and Kentucky in 1965, state teachers associations, with support of the NEA, won improvements in teaching conditions as well as in economic welfare after imposing sanctions state-wide. Many improvements in teaching conditions will be written into agreements reached by negotiation between school boards and teacher organizations. This will be stimulated by the rivalry of the NEA and its affiliates with teachers' unions of the American Federation of Teachers. There will probably continue to be an atmosphere typified by the concept "Anything you can do I can do better."

5. Improvement of School Administrators

Studies have shown that the working climate in a school or school system depends to a great extent upon the competence of the administrators. Higher standards of preparation of school administrators at all levels and greater opportunities for in-service development promise to produce administrators sensitive to teacher and student needs and capable of taking appropriate action to fulfill those needs.

6. Development of Grievance Machinery

Almost every sizable school system is likely to establish formal procedures for handling alleged unfair treatment of personnel. Such machinery will be used only in relatively few cases when differences cannot be resolved informally; but the existence of clear-cut, written policies will tend to reduce arbitrary or unfair practices.

What Teachers Can and Should Do About Conditions of Work

All of the roles of teachers required for maintenance of economic welfare, as listed in the preceding chapter, apply also to maintenance of a desirable working climate; but many policies and practices related to the working climate are determined at levels closer to the teacher than matters affecting economic welfare.

1. Group Action

a. There are opportunities at the school level, working directly with other teachers and the principal, to establish many aspects of a desirable work climate. Some such activities may be co-sponsored by teacher organizations, such as the programs conducted by the Time to Teach Project sponsored by the NEA Department of Classroom Teachers and local education associations.

b. As negotiation and grievance procedures are established in more school systems it will become increasingly important for teachers to be familiar with those procedures and how to use them.

c. Many activities to improve conditions of work do not involve formal organizations of teachers. They are carried out under the leadership of the principal, superintendent, supervisor, or teacher committees of a school or school system.

2. Individual Action

Several aspects of teaching conditions are controllable to a high degree by the individual teacher. Following are a few examples:

a. One means of reducing misassignment of teachers is for individual teachers to turn down employment requiring them to teach school subjects or levels in which they are not qualified. Just as a chemical engineer would not attempt to do the work of a civil engineer except in dire emergency, an English teacher should not attempt to teach math if he is not competent in that field.

b. Teachers need to know what the best instructional materials are in their respective fields and then proceed to request those materials from those responsible for their procurement. Often the application of persistence, specificity of requests, and good timing in relation to budget periods succeed in procuring teaching aids which would not be obtained if teachers waited passively for materials to be handed to them by the school administration.

c. Sometimes the real reason for allegedly poor teaching conditions lies in lack of ability or of appropriate preparation of the individual teacher. Teachers who are unhappy in their work should attempt to analyze their own competence objectively and seek self-improvement if necessary.

Chapter 11

Professional Organizations

Group professional responsibilities of teachers are fulfilled through various agencies in many different ways, but the preceding review of nine areas of professional concern leaves little doubt that professional organizations are by far the most important agencies through which teachers do collectively what is impossible for them to do individually.

Before a teacher can help maintain effective professional organizations he must decide which organizations to join and support. In some situations this is a difficult problem and requires much knowledge of the types of organizations and of their objectives, methods, activities, dues, and achievements. Education has more organizations than any other occupational field. There are over one thousand state, regional, and national organizations in education and about ten thousand local associations.

Major types of such organizations may be classified as follows: (1) general purpose, embracing most interests of the teaching profession; (2) special interest, related to subject field, teaching level, or type of position; and (3) honorary or fraternal societies.

In addition there are teachers' unions which are usually classified separately.

General purpose organizations may be further divided into three categories: (1) all-inclusive, enrolling all types of educators —classroom teachers, administrators, and others—in one single organization; (2) all-inclusive, but with departments according to special interests; and (3) separate organizations according to occupational position.

The multiplicity of organizations is not quite as chaotic as it seems when one learns that approximately ninety percent of all public school educators are indirectly associated with the all-inclusive national organization, the National Education Association, through membership in departments and in state and local affiliates of the NEA; and slightly more than half of all public school teachers are directly enrolled as NEA members.

Although many teacher organizations overlap or compete with each other for members, there is little open antagonism except between the American Federation of Teachers and the National Education Association, including its state and local affiliates. In 1966, the AFT had in its membership only seven percent of instructional staff of the public schools in the United States but, with backing of the AFL-CIO, the Federation was actively engaged in trying to win the majority of teachers away from the NEA and its affiliates. In the future it is likely that many teachers will be faced with choosing between the rival organizations. To make a wise choice teachers should be familiar with historical highlights of the development of teacher organizations, their current objectives and status, major issues, and the outlook for the future.

History of Professional Organizations

1. Origins of the National Education Association

a. Local general-purpose teacher associations may be traced back at least to 1794 when the Society of Associated Teachers was organized in New York City. Early local associations of teachers served primarily to provide for fellowship, in-service growth of teachers, improvement of the school curriculum and methods of teaching, and financial assistance to teachers in times of sickness or retirement. There is little evidence of significant influence of local teacher organizations in improving financial support and conditions of teaching until the advent of state teachers associations.

b. The first state teachers' associations were established in the 1840's. By 1857, eighteen states had established state associations of teachers. The state associations emerged to be the most influential type of organization, partly because the most crucial legislation affecting public education had been at the state level.

c. In 1857, ten state teachers' associations initiated a meeting in Philadelphia at which the NEA was established. It was first called the National Teachers' Association. The name National Education Association of the United States was adopted in 1906 when it was chartered by act of Congress.

(1) The prime initiators of the national association were relatively humble "practical teachers" rather than well-known or highly placed leaders. The two men primarily responsible for the first meeting were Thomas W. Valentine and Daniel B. Hagar, presidents, respectively, of the state associations of New York and Massachusetts. Valentine was a grammar-school teacher in Brooklyn and Hagar was principal of the Normal School at Salem, Massachusetts. However, famous educational leaders such as Horace Mann and Henry Barnard soon joined and became active in the Association.

(2) The purposes of the National Teachers' Association were stated in its first constitution: "To elevate the character and advance the interests of the profession of teaching, and to promote the cause of popular education in the United States." These basic purposes of what is now the NEA have remained the same until the present.

(3) For at least the first thirty years, the major activity of the National Teachers' Association was the exchange of ideas in speeches and discussions at the annual convention. Although now overshadowed by other activities of the NEA, the annual meetings remain a major educational forum. Recorded in the annual volumes of the NEA *Addresses and Proceedings* are thousands of speeches in which one can read the history of the problems, aspirations, and achievements of American education. Speakers have included almost all presidents of the

United States since the last quarter of the nineteenth century as well as such educational greats as Horace Mann and John Dewey.

2. The Era of Influence by Committee Pronouncement

From its founding by forty-three educators in 1857 until the end of World War I, the organization that is now the NEA remained a relatively small organization. By 1917, the NEA had only 8,500 members. Its leadership was dominated by college professors and school and college administrators. During the late nineteenth and early twentieth century the pronouncements of various blue ribbon, special committees had major influence on the development of American education. Some of the most influential committees are listed below:

Committee of Ten on Secondary School Studies, 1892-93
Committee of Fifteen on Elementary Education, 1893-95
Committee of Twelve on Rural Schools, 1895
Committees on College Entrance Requirements, 1899-1911.
Commission on the Reorganization of Secondary Education, 1913-21.

The seven cardinal principles of education advocated by the above named commission are listed in the chapter of this book on goals of education.

3. The Broadening Base of NEA Membership

a. After 1917, the NEA began a slow change from administrator-domination to classroom-teacher predominance. The influx of classroom teachers into membership swelled membership from 8,500 in 1917 to 53,000 in 1920, 216,000 in 1930, 454,000 in 1950, and about one million members by 1966.

b. Reasons for increasing classroom teacher membership and influence in the NEA include the following:

(1) The extension of political and other equal rights to women established a more favorable climate for participation of women teachers in affairs of the NEA and of state and local associations. The first woman president of the NEA, Ella Flagg Young of Chicago, was elected in 1910. This was ac-

complished only after a vigorous campaign and a vote from the floor in opposition to the candidate proposed by the majority of the nominating committee.

(2) Higher levels of preparation of teachers enabled many more teachers to hold their own in organizational contacts with administrators.

(3) Problems created by wartime neglect of the schools spurred teachers to attempt to improve their situation through teacher organizations.

(4) Competition of the American Federation of Teachers, organized in 1916, stimulated association leaders to attempt to enroll more teachers in membership and to give them a greater voice in the professional associations.

(5) The establishment of a permanent headquarters and staff of the NEA in Washington in 1917 led to great expansion of the association and increased effectiveness in pursuing goals of interest to classroom teachers.

(6) The creation of the Representative Assembly of the NEA in 1920 as the major governing body of the NEA encouraged widespread teacher interest in the NEA because delegates were selected by state and local associations.

(7) Beginning about 1910, and accelerating rapidly after 1920, the NEA began to play a major role in advancing teacher welfare as well as in the improvement of instruction.

(8) State and local associations increased their teacher membership and effective activities on behalf of teachers after 1910.

c. These listed developments led to the election of the first classroom teacher as president of the NEA in 1928. Classroom teachers have steadily gained in leadership, influence, and membership in the association since that time.

4. Development of State Education Associations

a. Between 1907 and 1925, the percent of eligible educators enrolled in state associations increased from fourteen to seventy-three percent. By 1966, approximately, ninety percent of the instructional staff in the United States was enrolled in state associations.

b. Prior to 1910, the principal activity of most state associations was to hold an annual convention. Only a few states employed staffs or maintained offices.

c. As membership and staffs of state associations grew, they became very effective in lobbying for favorable state legislation. Major legislative concerns and successes in most states included increased funds for all aspects of education, the establishment of state minimum salary laws, teacher tenure laws, teacher retirement provisions, and certification requirements.

5. Development of Local Education Associations

Until fairly recently local teacher organizations have been considered to be the weakest link in the chain of professional organizations.

a. Prior to the 1960's, few local associations employed staffs. Most had nominal dues, too low to support much of a program.

b. In many large cities which could have supported effective organizations, the splintering of teachers and administrators into many different local organizations rendered the organizations relatively ineffective. In New York City, for example, in the 1950's there were well over 100 different organizations of educators. Teachers were divided by teaching level, subjects taught, and even by religion.

c. Since 1960, many local associations have employed executive secretaries, broadened their programs, and increased cooperation with the state associations and the NEA. This vitalization of local education associations seems to be due in part to competition of teacher unions seeking to become exclusive bargaining agents for teachers. But even in school systems where there is no direct competition from teacher unions, local associations have been stimulated by success of strong, unified associations in winning increased support for education, improved teacher welfare, and better teaching conditions.

6. Development of Departments of the NEA

a. The development of NEA departments serving special interests of the teaching profession dates back to 1870. In that year the National Association of School Superintendents and the American

Normal School Association merged with the National Teachers' Association to form the National Educational Association. The two groups became the first departments of the NEA.

   b. Since 1870, a number of new departments were added to cover almost every major interest in education. Most departments were first established outside the NEA and later applied for admission. In some cases the NEA sponsored and subsidized new departments in fields where they seemed to be needed.

7. History of the American Federation of Teachers

   a. The American Federation of Teachers was organized in 1916 and affiliated the same year with the American Federation of Labor (AFL, now AFL-CIO). It was initiated by a few local organizations that had previously affiliated individually with organized labor.

   b. From its beginning the AFT differed from the NEA in at least three ways:

   (1) The AFT did not admit superintendents into membership and accepted principals and supervisors only under specified conditions.

   (2) It adopted many of the tenets of organized labor such as labor-management (teacher-administration) conflict of interests, and it adopted union procedures to achieve its objectives.

   (3) The AFT concentrated almost exclusively on teacher welfare and teaching conditions, while the NEA worked for improvement of instruction, professional standards, research, and professional ethics as well as for teacher welfare.

   c. Beginning with about 2,400 members in 1917, AFT membership spurted to 10,000 by 1920. However, membership dropped to 3,500 by 1925. This drop was caused in part by revitalization of program and vigorous recruitment activities of the NEA.

   d. Teacher union membership grew slowly after 1925 to reach about 61,000 by 1961. This membership constituted slightly less than 4 percent of the instructional staff of public schools.

   e. Beginning in the 1950's, the AFT began to get considerable help in money, manpower, and advice from the AFL-CIO, particularly the Industrial Union Department. This assistance was part of a comprehensive union drive to organize white collar workers, technicians, government employees, and salaried professional workers.

f. In 1961 the AFT achieved the greatest gain in its history. In that year the United Federation of Teachers, an AFT affiliate, won an election giving it the right to engage in collective bargaining with the school board on behalf of over 40,000 New York City teachers. This led to a gain of over 20,000 members in New York City alone by 1965.

(1) The New York City representation election was a psychological blow to the NEA, which supported a hastily and loosely organized coalition of dozens of non-union teacher organizations opposed to the AFT in the election.

(2) In the few years following the victory in New York City, AFT affiliates challenged NEA affiliates in a number of cities for the right to represent teachers in bargaining with school boards. In terms of numbers of elections won the NEA affiliates came out far ahead, but the AFT won most of the elections in the very largest city school systems where the NEA had not been very strong.

(3) By 1966, AFT locals had won representation rights in Detroit, Cleveland, and Boston and were engaged in an all-out war with NEA affiliates in a number of other cities. In that year total AFT membership reached 120,000.

8. Accomplishments of Teacher Organizations

a. Many of the accomplishments of the NEA and its affiliates in every aspect of teaching as a profession are described in the preceding chapters of this book and will not be repeated here except to conclude that practically every advance of the teaching profession has been led, stimulated, or supported by professional associations.

b. The AFT has not been large enough or powerful enough to build a record of accomplishment that can be evaluated at this time. But Federation spokesmen have declared that the very threat of unionization of teachers has stimulated administrators and school boards to improve teacher welfare and conditions of work and has stimulated professional associations to more militant activity.

Current Status of Professional Organizations

1. Purposes and Activities of the National Education Association

The NEA is the largest professional organization in the world. It serves almost all members of the teaching profession and works for improvement of almost all aspects of education, many of which have been described in this book. It would take more space than is available here even to list the complete variety of concerns and activities of the NEA and its affiliates. The scope of objectives of the NEA may be found in the Platform and Resolutions adopted each summer by the NEA Representative Assembly. These policy guidelines, details of the purposes and activities of the various national units and departments of the NEA, and a complete list of all state and local affiliates, are to be found in the latest edition of the annually-revised *NEA Handbook for Local, State, and National Associations.* Much of the following information is from the *NEA Handbook.* To organize one's concept of the NEA without getting lost in detail, it may be useful to consider the following outline of types of objectives of the NEA and means of achieving them.

a. Basic objectives of the NEA include:
  (1) High quality instruction
  (2) Favorable teaching conditions
  (3) Teacher welfare
  (4) Protection of rights of teachers
  (5) Professional standards
  (6) Active public support of education
  (7) Adequate facilities and materials.
b. Major means the NEA uses to achieve its objectives include:
  (1) Research
  (2) Publications
  (3) Press, radio, and television
  (4) Field services
  (5) Conventions
  (6) Legislative lobbying
  (7) Professional negotiation
  (8) Investigation reports
  (9) Sanctions.

2. Membership in the NEA

In 1966, there were approximately one million individual regular members of the NEA. The members include all types of educators —classroom teachers, school administrators, college professors and administrators, and specialists in schools, colleges, and educational agencies, both public and private. An estimated eighty-five to ninety per cent of all regular NEA members are classroom teachers. In addition to regular members (active, associate, life, and retired) the NEA membership includes about 120,000 student members. Annual dues for active members were $10 in 1966.

3. NEA Services to Members

a. All types of members receive nine issues of the *NEA Journal* annually and about twelve issues of the *NEA Reporter*.

(1) The *NEA Journal* contains articles to help improve instruction, improve teacher welfare, raise professional standards, and to keep up with new developments in education from kindergarten through college.

(2) The *NEA Reporter* is a professional newspaper that reports plans and activities of the NEA and its affiliates.

b. NEA members who are also members of their state association are entitled also to participate in money-saving optional economic welfare benefits made possible by the large size of the NEA membership. These programs include the following:

(1) Group life insurance

(2) Accident insurance

(3) Mutual investment fund

(4) Tax-sheltered annuities.

c. Active members may serve on NEA committees and commissions, participate in conferences, workshops, and the annual convention, receive consultant help by mail or in person, serve as delegates to the NEA from their local and state education associations, and directly, or through their representatives, have a voice in determining NEA policies.

d. The indirect benefits to the teaching profession and society stemming from NEA activities are probably even more significant than the direct benefits to members. NEA research, publications, films and filmstrips, conferences, press releases, radio and television programs establish a general climate favorable to education and provide specific information and stimulation used by local and state associations, colleges and universities, school boards, lay organizations, and governmental bodies. Many of the gains in advancing the status of the teaching profession and the cause of education, although directly achieved by other agencies, could not some to pass without the services available from the NEA.

4. How NEA Policy Is Determined

In effect, the NEA is governed by representatives of its state and local affiliates. Following are descriptions of the governing bodies:

a. *Representative Assembly.* The Representative Assembly is composed mainly of approximately 6,500 delegates sent by affiliated local and state associations to the annual meeting of the NEA. Delegates are allocated on the basis of the number of NEA members in each association. The budget, resolutions, recommendations, reports of officers and committees, and amendments to the Bylaws must be presented to the Representative Assembly for approval. The annual resolutions of this body establish policies which outline the general program and guide the activities of the officers and staff throughout the year. The Representative Assembly also elects the president and other major officers of the NEA.

b. *Board of Directors.* The Board of Directors is charged with looking after many aspects of Association affairs between meetings of the Representative Assembly and with making reports and recommendations to the Assembly. Each state is entitled to choose one or more directors, depending upon the number of NEA members in the state. State directors promote NEA membership and program in their respective states.

c. *Executive Committee.* The Executive Committee acts on behalf of the Board of Directors between meetings of the Board. The eleven-member Committee is composed of the major officers of the Association, the chairman of the Board of Trustees, two members elected by and from the Board of Directors, at least one of whom must be a classroom teacher, and four members elected at large by the Representative Assembly, at least two of whom must be classroom teachers.

d. *Board of Trustees.* The trustees' responsibilities are limited to appointment of the executive secretary of the Association and management of the permanent funds and properties of the Association.

5. Organizational Structure of the NEA

The NEA structure at the national level includes four types of permanent units: commissions (and council), committees, departments, and divisions. In addition, special projects of relatively short duration focus attention and action on crucial current problems. See the NEA Organizational Chart for the abbreviated names and relationships of these units.

a. *Commissions and Council.* Five commissions and one council operate in large areas of professional interest under the general supervision of the Executive Committee. These units conduct investigations, formulate proposed policies, recommend standards, disseminate information, build support for better programs of education, and work for safeguards necessary to protect freedom of teaching and learning.

b. *Committees.* Six standing committees of the NEA carry on continuous programs of study, interpretation, and action in the fields of citizenship, credit unions, educational travel, international relations, professional ethics, and educational finance. Six additional committees function in connection with the annual convention: Audit, Budget, Bylaws and Rules, Credentials, Elections, and Resolutions.

c. *Joint Committees.* The joint committee is one form of cooperation between the NEA and other organizations with mutual interests in specific problems.

d. *Departments.*

(1) Through thirty-three departments, the NEA meets many of the special needs of educators, as well as the general needs of education. Most departments fall into one of three categories: subject field, such as social studies or science; school level, such as elementary or higher education; and type of position, such as classroom teacher or administrator.

(2) Departments choose their own officers, plan their special-interest programs, and adopt policies which apply to their specialization. Except for the Department of Classroom Teachers and the National Association for Higher Education, all departments levy dues to support their programs. The departments receive free housing and other services from the NEA. All departments promote and urge NEA membership on the part of their members. Many of them require NEA membership.

(3) After a department has decided what ought to be done with respect to any problem in which it is especially interested, it may receive help in implementation from the NEA or other departments. Most of the relationships between the NEA and departments are voluntary and informal and depend to a great degree upon mutual interests and cooperation.

e. *Divisions.* Eighteen NEA divisions provide basic services such as research and publications for members, affiliates, and other NEA units and departments.

f. *Special Projects.* Special projects involving intensive programs of short duration focus NEA resources on selected programs of high current concern. Projects of recent years have dealt with juvenile delinquency, the academically talented, urban problems, instruction, time to teach, English composition, automation, and NEA development. Some of these projects have been financed in whole or part by philanthropic foundations. In addition, many special projects have been conducted by departments in their fields of interest.

g. *Consultants.* Several NEA consultants, who work with state and local associations and school systems and with individuals, operate directly from offices of some assistant executive secretaries of the NEA. Included are general field workers and consultants for such concerns as the improvement of instruction and salaries. However, most consultant services are provided by the staffs of departments and other units listed above.

h. *Regional NEA Offices.* Small staffs man regional field offices to bring NEA services closer to the membership and affiliated state and local associations. In 1966, there were such offices in or near Atlanta, Boston, Indianapolis, St. Paul, San Francisco, and Trenton. In addition, the Urban Services Division employs several

ORGANIZATION CHART

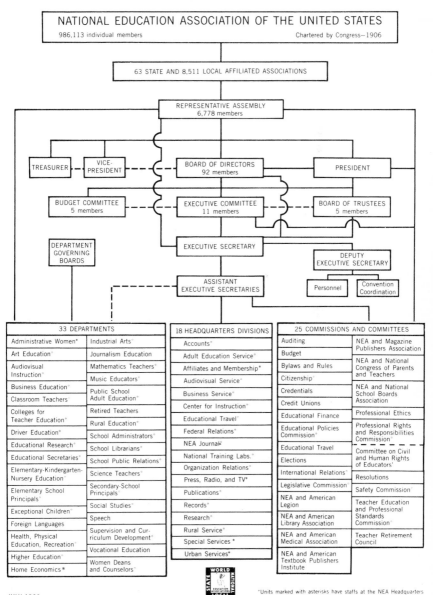

NATIONAL EDUCATION ASSOCIATION OF THE UNITED STATES
986,113 individual members   Chartered by Congress—1906

63 STATE AND 8,511 LOCAL AFFILIATED ASSOCIATIONS

REPRESENTATIVE ASSEMBLY
6,778 members

TREASURER   VICE-PRESIDENT   BOARD OF DIRECTORS 92 members   PRESIDENT

BUDGET COMMITTEE 5 members   EXECUTIVE COMMITTEE 11 members   BOARD OF TRUSTEES 5 members

DEPARTMENT GOVERNING BOARDS   EXECUTIVE SECRETARY

DEPUTY EXECUTIVE SECRETARY

ASSISTANT EXECUTIVE SECRETARIES   Personnel   Convention Coordination

33 DEPARTMENTS		18 HEADQUARTERS DIVISIONS	25 COMMISSIONS AND COMMITTEES	
Administrative Women*	Industrial Arts°	Accounts°	Auditing	NEA and Magazine Publishers Association
Art Education°	Journalism Education	Adult Education Service°	Budget	
Audiovisual Instruction°	Mathematics Teachers°	Affiliates and Membership*	Bylaws and Rules	NEA and National Congress of Parents and Teachers
	Music Educators°	Audiovisual Service°	Citizenship°	
Business Education°	Public School Adult Education°	Business Service°	Credentials	NEA and National School Boards Association
Classroom Teachers°		Center for Instruction°	Credit Unions	
Colleges for Teacher Education°	Retired Teachers	Educational Travel°	Educational Finance	Professional Ethics
	Rural Education°	Federal Relations°	Educational Policies Commission°	Professional Rights and Responsibilities Commission°
Driver Education°	School Administrators°	NEA Journal°		
Educational Research°	School Librarians°	National Training Labs.°	Educational Travel°	
Educational Secretaries°	School Public Relations°	Organization Relations°	Elections	Committee on Civil and Human Rights of Educators°
Elementary-Kindergarten-Nursery Education°	Science Teachers°	Press, Radio, and TV*	International Relations°	
Elementary School Principals°	Secondary-School Principals°	Publications°	Legislative Commission°	Resolutions
Exceptional Children°	Social Studies°	Records°	NEA and American Legion	Safety Commission°
Foreign Languages	Speech	Research°	NEA and American Library Association	Teacher Education and Professional Standards Commission°
Health, Physical Education, Recreation°	Supervision and Curriculum Development°	Rural Service°	NEA and American Medical Association	
	Vocational Education	Special Services *		Teacher Retirement Council
Higher Education°	Women Deans and Counselors°	Urban Services*	NEA and American Textbook Publishers Institute	
Home Economics*				

JULY 1966

°Units marked with asterisks have staffs at the NEA Headquarters

107

field workers at these and other locations to render special help to large urban associations.

i. *DuShane Defense Fund and Fund for Teacher Rights.* These two funds, described in the preceding chapter on conditions of work, are administered separately from the units described above. Requests for use of these funds to aid individual teachers are usually made through local and state associations.

6. Staff of the NEA

The NEA and its affiliated departments employ over 1,100 persons, most of whom work in or from the NEA Headquarters Building in Washington, D.C. Many of the professional personnel on these staffs are former teachers. In addition many are specialists in functions such as writing and editing, public relations, statistics and research, curriculum, and business management. The chief administrative officer of the Association is the executive secretary, appointed by the Board of Trustees for a term of four years.

7. State Education Associations

a. There are statewide professional associations of teachers in every state, territory, commonwealth, and in the District of Columbia. They hold conferences and conventions, work for favorable legislation, issue publications, assist local education associations— all in terms of the needs of education and the profession within their respective states. They elect their officers, approve policies, and manage their own affairs. Their affiliation with the NEA permits them to send delegates to the NEA Representative Assembly, to receive various kinds of assistance from the NEA, and to cooperate closely in advancing education and the interests and goals of all professional teachers.

b. State associations, even when they are called "teachers' associations," include all kinds of educators in their membership. Many have active department programs. The annual conventions or district conventions of most state associations are considered to be so valuable in the in-service education of teachers that schools are closed for one or two days to allow teachers to attend.

c. Many state associations offer free or low-cost liability insurance and low-cost automobile, life, and other types of insurance.

d. The effectiveness of state associations varies greatly for a variety of reasons. One indication of great differences in programs is the great variation in annual dues which range from $4 to $39 annually.

e. In 1966, a total of about 1300 persons were employed on the full-time staffs of state associations. About 450 of these may be classified as professional personnel. In addition, literally thousands of teachers work on committees, as officers, or in other leadership capacities.

8. Local Associations Affiliated with NEA

More than 8200 local education associations were affiliated with the NEA in 1966. These range in size from a single school faculty to large city or county associations enrolling many thousands of teachers. Following are some of the characteristics of such associations.

a. The pattern of organization varies greatly and is not prescribed by the NEA. Some are all-inclusive, others include separate departments within an all-inclusive organization, and some are separate organizations of groups such as classroom teachers and principals. Relationships of local organizations with state associations range from complete independence to complete structural integration as a unit of the state association.

b. The scope of activity and effectiveness of local associations varies greatly from very narrow, ineffective programs to extremely broad and influential associations concerned with improving education as well as the welfare of teachers. Dues vary likewise from almost nothing to $35 or more per year.

c. In negotiating with school boards for improved conditions, the local association is the key agency, although it may receive considerable assistance and support from the state association and the NEA.

d. A growing number of larger local associations are employing full-time executive secretaries and other staff. In 1966, about 90 local associations employed a total of over 200 persons.

e. Over ninety per cent of all public school teachers in the United States belong to a local education association.

9. Independent Special Interest Organizations

Although most teaching subjects, levels, and types of educational positions are served by some NEA department or unit, there are some sizeable independent special-interest organizations. Some overlap with NEA departments and a few have no counterparts in the NEA. Some of the most significant independent national organizations are listed below, in alphabetical order.

American Association of University Professors
American Personnel and Guidance Association
American Vocational Association
Association for Childhood Educational International
National Council of Teachers of English

10. The American Federation of Teachers

Many educators do not consider the AFT to be a "professional association" and, indeed, the AFT to date has not assumed more than a few of the professional responsibilities described in this book. Nevertheless, the AFT avows broad objectives not greatly different from those of the NEA. The major differences are in the pattern of organization, methods of achieving objectives, scope of program, and affiliation with organized labor. Major aspects of the status of the AFT follow.

a. Membership is concentrated in relatively few large urban centers.

(1) New York City alone accounted for about one-fourth of the estimated national membership of 120,000 in 1966.

(2) About half of the total national membership is concentrated in eight cities: Chicago, Cleveland, Detroit, Gary, Los Angeles, Milwaukee, New York, and Philadelphia.

(3) Nationwide there were about 600 locals in 1966.

b. The organizational structure of the AFT is tightly unified. When a teacher joins a local unit he automatically becomes a member of the national and state federation if there is one in his state, and, indirectly, a member of the AFL-CIO Industrial Union Department.

c. Total annual dues ranged in 1966 from $18 to $60. The national AFT share was set at $12 effective in 1967.

d. The weakest level in the AFT structure is the state federation. Only about twenty-seven states had state federations at all in 1966, and most of these were relatively inactive.

e. The major means by which the AFT pursues its objectives are collective bargaining and strikes.

f. The AFT is pledged to support labor unions. In return the AFL-CIO and some constituent unions provide financial assistance, manpower, advice, and political influence on behalf of the AFT.

11. Professional Fraternities, Sororities, and Societies

Several professional fraternities, sororities, and societies contribute toward advancement of the teaching profession as well as toward fellowship. Some publish journals and other publications, conduct professional programs and conferences, and stimulate the conduct of research and dissemination of its findings.

a. The largest and most influential is the 60,000-member fraternity Phi Delta Kappa. Its journal, the *Phi Delta Kappan,* is noted as a forum for discussion of controversial issues in education. In addition it fosters the conduct of research through special publications, conferences, and other means.

b. Kappa Delta Pi, an honorary society, publishes the periodical, *Educational Forum.*

c. The best-known woman's organization is the Delta Kappa Gamma Society.

d. The National Society for the Study of Education is a small but influential group composed primarily of college professors. Its major activity is preparation of scholarly yearbooks.

12. World Confederation of Organizations of the Teaching Profession

The WCOTP is an international organization devoted to improvement of education, teacher status, and international understanding. It is comprised of national teacher organizations of about eighty-five countries of the world. State and local associations may affiliate on an associate basis.

Problems and Issues in Professional Organizations

1. Lack of Adequate Unity of Teachers

The unity of the teaching profession varies greatly among states and school systems. Generally organizations are more successful in advancing the morale, status, and welfare of teachers and the quality of education where most educators are members of the same general purpose organizations. The ability of educators to achieve maximum possible advancement of their status is probably hampered by the following divisive factors:

a. The struggle between the AFT and NEA affiliates in some school systems

b. The lack of fully unified membership and program of the NEA-related associations in many states and at the national level

c. The large number of independent organizations, some overlapping and competing with each other

d. The differences that exist among elementary school teachers, secondary school teachers, and those at the college level

e. The great diversity of professional, social, political, and intellectual backgrounds and outlook among individuals in the teaching profession

f. The lack of adequate provision in some all-inclusive organizations for balance of influence and interests of different groups of educators within the organization, particularly classroom teachers and administrators

g. The lack of an all-inclusive organization at all in some school systems

h. The "freeloaders" who do not join or support any of the organizations working on their behalf.

2. Lack of Adequate Numbers of Trained Association Leaders and Staff

The rapid growth of teacher organizations has outstripped the supply of qualified leaders and staff specialists. Brief leadership programs and staff workshops have been conducted by teacher organizations, but, in 1966, there was not a single college or university program to specifically prepare persons for organization work, except for some short-term workshops on professional negotiations and collective bargaining.

3. Is It Desirable for Teachers to Be Affiliated with Unions?

    a. Arguments for affiliation with labor unions declare that:

      (1) Labor union policies and practices are applicable to teachers because they work for fixed remuneration from employers.

      (2) Labor unions generally support the extension and improvement of public education.

      (3) Teacher unions receive direct support from other unions.

      (4) Support of the labor union movement is a desirable social objective.

      (5) Labor unions win greater gains in money and teaching conditions than do professional associations.

    b. Arguments against affiliation with labor unions declare that:

      (1) Teaching is a unique profession to which labor union philosophy does not apply. In most school systems there is less difference in the outlook of teachers and administrators than between workers and management in industry.

      (2) Education serves all segments of society. Affiliation with organized labor may, in the long run, reduce school support by the general public.

      (3) The interests of labor unions may run counter to the interests of education and teachers. Labor unions have often opposed taxes needed for school support.

      (4) Support of strikes by other unions can interfere with education. For example, in 1965 and 1966, the AFT conducted an active campaign to boycott some major textbooks and encyclopedias because they were produced in a plant struck by a printers' union.

      (5) In the past decade, NEA-affiliated associations have won greater salary gains than has the AFT in its areas of predominance and greater gains than won by most industrial unions.

4. Should Teachers Strike?

Although most teachers and other citizens do not favor strikes by teachers under any circumstances, a number of local teacher organizations have resorted to brief work stoppages when frustrated in achieving their objectives.

   a. The following are arguments in favor of teacher strikes.

     (1) Strikes by organized labor have been successful in industry in winning representation rights, economic benefits, and other advances.

     (2) Strikes are invoked only under extreme circumstances.

     (3) Gains won by strikes outweigh possible harm to the students and the public image of the teacher.

     (4) Brief strikes do less harm to the educational program than the possible alternative of long-term sanctions of a school system.

   b. The following are arguments against teacher strikes.

     (1) Strikes by teachers are usually illegal or unethical.

     (2) Teacher strikes are upsetting to students.

     (3) Strikes build public ill will and loss of respect for teachers.

     (4) In the long run measures such as public-information programs, political action, and, in extreme cases, professional sanctions, achieve greater gains than strikes.

The Outlook for Teacher Organizations

1. Growing Importance of Associations

Teacher organizations will likely play an even more important role in the future than in the past. One reason is the likelihood that most school systems will have some kind of negotiation agreement with local teacher organizations. Teacher associations also seem to be pointing toward greater activity in improving instruction.

2. Expanded Roles of Local and National Associations

Although state associations will remain important, the roles of local and national organizations will be more significant than in the past because of:

   a. The urbanization and consolidation of school systems

b. The employment of staffs by large local associations

c. The increasing national interest in and financial support of education.

3. Continuation of AFT-NEA Struggle

The competition of the NEA and AFT for the allegiance of teachers will probably continue during the foreseeable future.

a. The AFT will probably continue to gain members in areas dominated economically and politically by labor unions but is not likely to enroll more than a small part of teachers nationwide.

b. Competition for membership will make the AFT and NEA more like each other, with teacher unions seeking to expand their programs beyond teacher welfare and NEA and affiliates pursuing teacher welfare with greater militancy.

c. A higher proportion of teachers will belong to and participate in professional organizations.

4. Reorganization of NEA

The NEA is likely, as it has several times in its history, to re-organize in response to changing conditions. It will probably tighten unity and relationships with its local, state, and departmental affiliates to achieve greater efficiency and effectiveness. Merger, in 1966, of the NEA with the formerly all-Negro American Teachers Association will probably stimulate accelerated unification of the remaining racially-segregated state and local associations in some southern states.

5. Expanding Need for Association Staff Members

The increased activities of teacher organizations are likely to stimulate planned preparation for professional association work as a recognized career field.

What Teachers Can and Should Do About Professional Organizations

1. Choose Organizations to Join

To make a wise choice of organizations teachers should evaluate the philosophy, objectives, program, and achievements of each organization he considers.

2. Participate Actively

If democratic values and professional status of teachers are to be maintained and advanced, each teacher needs to do more than merely pay dues. He should become familiar with current organizational programs and problems; attend meetings and help to frame policies; and serve on committees or in other capacities if called upon to do so.

3. Suggest and Support Necessary Changes

No human institution is perfect. Also, it is common for organizations to lag behind rapidly changing conditions. Rather than condemn, or blindly support all aspects of the status quo, teachers need to continually evaluate, initiate, support or help implement necessary changes in organizational structure and program.

4. Prepare for Leadership Roles

Increasing numbers of teachers should seek informal and formal preparation for positions of leadership or full-time employment in professional organizations.

Glossary

Academic freedom: the right of teachers to teach the truth as they see it.

Accreditation: a process whereby a recognized agency evaluates and approves the program and facilities of educational institutions according to specified standards.

Action research: a procedure in which classroom teachers are directly involved in identifying problems, forming hypotheses, experimenting with new approaches, and applying research findings.

Certification: the process of giving legal approval to an individual to practice his profession, usually by a state agency.

Collective bargaining: formal negotiation, according to written procedures, between representatives of a group of employees and their employers regarding compensation and conditions of work. Usually follows procedures governing labor unions under state and federal law.

Fringe benefits: benefits to employees other than salary. (Usually this definition includes retirement benefits which are treated separately in this book because of their major importance to teachers.)

Grievance: a complaint of alleged unjust treatment that, in the opinion of an employee, fails to receive adequate or just consideration through normal administrative channels.

Index salary schedule: a salary schedule in which all levels and steps are stated in terms of ratio to a base salary.

Merit pay: extra pay to teachers judged to be outstandingly effective in their work.

Professional autonomy: the right of individual members of a profession and the profession as a group to make decisions regarding appropriate aspects of professional procedures and standards.

Professional ethics: a widely accepted code of professional behavior designed to protect both the public and members of the profession from improper conduct.

Professional negotiation: negotiation, according to formal procedures, of teacher associations and school boards regarding economic welfare and teaching conditions. Usually follows procedures especially developed for teachers under state law or local agreement.

Professional sanctions: as used in education it usually refers to censure of a school system by a professional association or associations for maintaining highly undesirable conditions. Sanctions may be applied in various ways ranging from a simple public statement to the recommendation that teachers refrain from accepting employment in a school system under sanction.

Single salary schedule: a schedule which bases salary only upon preparation and experience. There is no differential based upon sex, grade level taught, or quality of teaching.

Tenure: the right to maintain a position until retirement unless proven to have demonstrated gross misconduct or inefficiency as defined by law, regulation, or contract.

Bibliography

Books

American Federation of Teachers, Commission on Educational Reconstruction, *Organizing the Teaching Profession*. Glencoe, Ill.: Free Press, 1955. 320 pp.

Armstrong, W. Earl and T. M. Stinnett, *A Manual on Certification Requirements for School Personnel in the United States,* 1964 ed. Washington, D.C.: National Commission on Teacher Education and Professional Standards, National Education Association, 1964. 223 pp.

Barnes, Fred P., *Research for the Practitioner in Education*. Washington, D.C.: Department of Elementary School Principals, National Education Association, 1964. 141 pp.

California Teachers Association, Commission on Teacher Education and Professional Standards, *Teacher Competence: Its Nature and Scope*. Burlingame, Calif.: the Association, 1957. 48 pp.

Conant, James B., *The Education of American Teachers*. New York: McGraw-Hill Book Company, 1963. 275 pp.

Conant, James B., *Shaping Educational Policy*. New York: McGraw-Hill Book Company, 1964. 139 pp.

Educational Policies Commission of the American Association of School Administrators and the National Education Association, *The Central Purpose of American Education*. Washington, D.C.: the Commission, 1961. 21 pp.

Harris, Chester W., ed., *Encyclopedia of Educational Research*. 3rd ed. New York: The Macmillan Company, 1960. 1,564 pp.

Kinney, Lucien B., *Certification in Education*. Englewood Cliffs, N.J.: Prentice-Hall, Inc., 1964. 178 pp.

Kleinmann, Jack H., *Fringe Benefits for Public School Personnel*. New York: Bureau of Publications, Teachers College, Columbia University, 1962. 178 pp.

Lieberman, Myron, *Education as a Profession*. Englewood Cliffs, N.J.: Prentice-Hall, Inc., 1956. 540 pp.

Lieberman, Myron, *The Future of Public Education*. Chicago: The University of Chicago Press, 1960. 294 pp.

National Education Association, *NEA Handbook for Local, State, and National Associations*. Washington, D.C.: the Association, new edition published each fall. Approx. 480 pp.

National Education Association, Committee on Professional Ethics, *Opinions of the Committee on Professional Ethics,* 1966 ed. Washington, D.C.: the Association, 1966. 115 pp.

National Education Association, Department of Classroom Teachers, *Innovations for Time to Teach*. Washington, D.C.: the Department, 1966. 147 pp.

National Education Association, Department of Classroom Teachers, "What Research Says to the Teacher" series. Washington, D.C.: the Department. 32 pp. booklets. 33 booklets in series.

National Education Association, National Commission on Teacher Education and Professional Standards, *New Horizons for the Teaching Profession,* ed. Margaret Lindsey. Washington, D.C.: the Commission, 1961. 243 pp.

National Education Association, National Commission on Teacher Education and Professional Standards, *A Position Paper on Teacher Education and Professional Standards*. Washington, D.C.: the Commission, 1963. 33 pp.

National Education Association, Project on Instruction, *Schools for the Sixties*. New York: McGraw-Hill Book Company, 1963. 146 pp.

National Education Association, Research Division, "Reports." Some 15 reports of major Research Division studies published annually.

Riccio, Anthony C. and Frederick R. Cyphert, eds., *Teaching in America*. Columbus, Ohio. Charles E. Merrill Publishing Company, 1962. 528 pp.

Shumsky, Abraham, *The Action Research Way of Learning: An Approach to In-Service Education*. New York: Bureau of Publications, Teachers College, Columbia University, 1958. 210 pp.

Stiles, Lindley J., and others, *Teacher Education in the United States*. New York: Ronald Press, 1960.

Stinnett, T. M., Jack H. Kleinmann, and Martha L. Ware, *Professional Negotiation in Public Education*. New York: The Macmillan Company, 1966. 309 pp.

Stinnett, T. M. and Albert J. Huggett, *Professional Problems of Teachers,* 2nd ed. New York: The Macmillan Company, 1963. 516 pp.

Wesley, Edgar B., *NEA: The First Hundred Years*. New York: Harper & Row, Publishers, 1957. 419 pp.

Periodicals

American Federationist. American Federation of Teachers (monthly during school year).

Changing Education. American Federation of Teachers (quarterly).

Journal of Teacher Education. National Commission for Teacher Education and Professional Standards, NEA (quarterly).

NEA Journal. National Education Association (monthly, Sept.-May).

NEA Reporter. National Education Association (12 issues).
NEA Research Bulletin. Research Division, NEA (4 times a year).
Phi Delta Kappan. Phi Delta Kappa (monthly).
Review of Educational Research. American Educational Research Association, NEA (5 issues).
Student NEA News. National Commission on Teacher Education and Professional Standards (a few times a year).
Teachers College Record. Teachers College, Columbia University (monthly, Oct.-May).

Unpublished Doctoral Dissertations

Dorros, Sidney, "The Identification of Learnings Needed by Experienced Public-School Teachers to Fulfill Their Group Professional Responsibilities." The George Washington University, 1965.

Faust, Wilda F., "The Readiness of First-Year Degree Teachers for Professional Organizations: A Comparative Study of Members and Non-Members of the Student National Education Association." The George Washington University, 1961.

Groebli, John M., "National Organizations in the Education Profession at Mid-Twentieth Century: Present Status and Future Development." George Peabody College for Teachers, 1958.

MacCracken, Elliott B., "The Preparation of Teachers for Membership in the Profession." Stanford University, 1953.

Randall, Gerald A., "Grievance Procedures for Public School Professional Personnel." Teachers College, Columbia University, 1960.

Sies, Luther F., "The Number, Intensity, and Persistence of Professional Problems of Beginning Elementary School Teachers as Related to Patterns of Teacher Preparation." The George Washington University, 1962.

Smith, Richard A., "Maturity of Education as a Profession." Stanford University, 1956.

Vanderpool, Julius Alden, "The Profession of Education." Stanford University, 1957.

Wolpert, Arnold W., "A Survey and Analysis of the Status, Problems, and Potential of Teaching as a Profession." University of Southern California, 1960.

Index

587